HEAL YOUR
POWER
HEAL YOUR
LIFE

Essential Healing Strategies
for Women on the Rise

LANE L. COBB, MS, CPC

BALBOA.
PRESS
A DIVISION OF HAY HOUSE

Balboa Press books may be ordered through booksellers or by contacting:

Balboa Press
A Division of Hay House
1663 Liberty Drive
Bloomington, IN 47403
www.balboapress.com
1 (877) 407-4847

Because of the dynamic nature of the Internet, any web addresses or links contained in this book may have changed since publication and may no longer be valid. The views expressed in this work are solely those of the author and do not necessarily reflect the views of the publisher, and the publisher hereby disclaims any responsibility for them.

The author of this book does not dispense medical advice or prescribe the use of any technique as a form of treatment for physical, emotional, or medical problems without the advice of a physician, either directly or indirectly. The intent of the author is only to offer information of a general nature to help you in your quest for emotional and spiritual well-being. In the event you use any of the information in this book for yourself, which is your constitutional right, the author and the publisher assume no responsibility for your actions.

Any people depicted in stock imagery provided by Thinkstock are models, and such images are being used for illustrative purposes only. Certain stock imagery © Thinkstock.

Print information available on the last page.

ISBN: 978-1-5043-5832-3 (sc)
ISBN: 978-1-5043-5833-0 (e)

Library of Congress Control Number: 2016908582

Balboa Press rev. date: 11/21/2016

Contents

Dedication

This book is dedicated to the women it was meant to help – women of all ages, races, and backgrounds, without whom this world would cease to exist, but who often forget that they are divinely gifted and powerful beyond measure.

I thank my family, and especially my husband, who has championed me through my healing process and who has generously allowed me to share with readers information about our relationship, in the interest of contributing to those in need of healing and for whom relationships are of special interest.

Foreword

By The Reverend Lameteria D. Hall

When I met Lane Cobb, I had been dealing with some life issues that had weighed me down for many years. After just one coaching session with Lane, I experienced the freedom that I had been craving. I liken the experience to a "spiritual jumpstart"; a renewed ability to be and do that which I love and to have that which I now believe I deserve. Lane helped me to peel away the layers of emotional baggage that had plagued me since childhood, and for the first time, I felt truly connected to my true power and my divine self-expression. As a result of my session with Lane, I was inspired to purchase her book, and I am honored to have been chosen to provide the foreword for its 2nd edition. *Heal Your Power, Heal Your Life* is an inspiration and an invitation to women everywhere to Heal, Grow, and Thrive! It truly has set me free to be my truest most authentic self, to uncover my unique gifts, and to share the gift that I am with the world through my ministry of service.

In this book, Lane demonstrates her wisdom and passion for empowering women to know their true power. A GPS (Global Positioning System) is a technological tool that helps us navigate from one place to another in the world. Lane has provided us with an HPS (Healing Power System), giving us tools that we can use to navigate through our journey of emotional and spiritual healing, each at our own pace. With this system of guiding principles, Lane supports us in merging every aspect of our lives so that we can express our true greatness in the world. Her simple message to all of us is Heal, Grow, and Thrive!

Through the genius of this wonderful book, Lane has created a series of mini spiritual retreats. Each healing practice offers readers an opportunity to expand their thinking and experience a transformation of the body, mind, and spirit to live a healthier, happier, and more audacious lifestyle. Each chapter takes you on a true-hearted journey of self-exploration that places you firmly on the path of self-love and self-actualization.

Heal Your Power, Heal Your Life is a must read for *women on the rise* and for any woman who is committed to living life on purpose! My hope for all who read this book is that they experience the peace of mind that comes with self-love and self-acceptance, and the courage to share their greatness with the world. Lane has inspired me to thrive in the valleys and soar over the mountain tops of my life with fresh insight and a new appreciation for who I am and what I am here to accomplish. Thank you, Lane, for leading the way!

Reverend Lameteria D. Hall is an Ordained Licensed Minister for The Universal Foundation for Better Living, Inc. and the Dean of Teacher Training at the Johnnie Colemon Theological Seminary. She resides in Baltimore, MD.

Introduction

When I was writing this book, I knew that I was writing for the purpose of empowering women everywhere to know their true power, to love themselves, and honor themselves as special, unique, and gifted. I want women to know that they are worthy and that they can be, do, and have everything and anything they set their mind to and are willing to work for. As a spiritual empowerment coach for women, I know the first thing we must do is believe in ourselves, to nurture ourselves, and to step into our own greatness.

I have dedicated much of my life to helping people understand their motivations; why they think, feel and behave the way they do, and what the consequences of those thoughts, feelings, and behaviors are. As an intuitive healer and coach, I've had the privilege of helping women (and some men) work through their emotional blocks so they can be, do, and have more of what they really want in life. In this book, I will share with you some of the healing practices that I, not only teach my clients, but also use in my own life to transcend my self-imposed limitations and stay true to myself. What you'll find is that many, if not all, of the practices in the book are inter-related, and all have a deeply spiritual context. By allowing yourself to see beneath the surface of your life, you will also connect with your inner wisdom and honor the purpose for which you were born. I firmly believe that there is a power greater than ourselves that is working for our good and guiding us toward our highest intention. As you work through the information contained in these pages, it will be important for you to honor that part of yourself and be patient with yourself. Transformation is a process, and it's not one size fits all.

So, whether you're a beginner on the path to healing and empowerment or a seasoned traveler, you'll do well to remember that listening to yourself and taking care of yourself are key to that process. You can only be as powerful as you allow yourself to be and it's important that you allow yourself to see who you are being and experience what you are feeling at any moment. Along your empowerment journey, you will be met with thoughts, feelings, and emotions that may threaten to distract you. These are opportunities for you to step into your power and move in the direction you have envisioned for your life.

Even the most powerful people are sometimes held back by unresolved issues and emotional baggage. *Heal Your*

Power, Heal Your Life gives you tools and practices to help you shed your emotional baggage, shift your mindset and stand in your greatness now!

So as you read this book, I invite you to give yourself permission to be fully who you are. Honor yourself enough to know that what you think is important, and love yourself enough to let yourself want what you want. And most of all, remember that you are worthy and capable of having absolutely anything that you are willing to work for!

At the end of each chapter, I have suggested actions that you can take to integrate that chapter's lessons into your life. I also suggest that you take some time to complete the Healing Questions section of each chapter before moving onto the next one, in order to increase your self-awareness and amplify the transformational energy contained in these pages. If you would like to expand your understanding of any of the concepts that are included in the book, visit me on my website and take advantage of some of the materials you find there. There's also a contact page in case you would like to reach me directly.

It is my pleasure and my purpose to educate and empower women to heal, grow, and thrive, and I am honored to have an opportunity to support you in this process. May you be blessed by the lessons contained in this book, and may you continue to seek out opportunities to bring transformation into your life as frequently and in as many ways as possible.

In loving gratitude,

Coach Lane

"Our deepest fear is not that we are inadequate. Our deepest fear is that we are powerful beyond measure. It is our light, not our darkness that most frightens us. We ask ourselves, 'Who am I to be brilliant, gorgeous, talented, fabulous?' Actually, who are you not to be? You are a child of God. Your playing small does not serve the world. There is nothing enlightened about shrinking so that other people won't feel insecure around you. We are all meant to shine, as children do. We were born to make manifest the glory of God that is within us. It's not just in some of us; it's in everyone. And as we let our own light shine, we unconsciously give other people permission to do the same. As we are liberated from our own fear, our presence automatically liberates others."

– Marianne Williamson, *A Return to Love: Reflections on the Principles of "A Course in Miracles"*

What is a Healing Practice?

A healing practice, among other things, is a way of thinking, acting, or behaving that facilitates a shift in energy, helps us grow and develop as human beings and connects us with our divine essence. In our lives, we all experience things that shape us in one way or another and that give us, not only our sense of who we are for ourselves, but who we are for the world and who the world is for us. In essence, a human being's reality is shaped by his or her experiences; those experiences imprint us with their energetic signatures, and it behooves us to make ourselves aware of those imprints – their origins and effects – if we are to have access to our true selves.

His Holiness The 14th Dalai Lama, Tenzin Gyatso is quoted as saying – *"How you do anything is how you do everything"*. This means that how you think, feel, and act in one area of your life affects every other area of your life. This is important to remember. Often people believe their attitudes and behaviors in one aspect of their lives won't affect any other aspect, save that one. This couldn't be any farther from the truth! Everything you think, feel, and do affects every part of your life, and taking on just one of these healing practices can positively impact your entire life, if you are open to it. But, you must be consistent. Your personal power is a function of your intention. If your intention is to live a powerful and enlightened life, that is exactly what you will do.

It's also important that you understand that personal empowerment is a multifaceted, multilevel process, and you are equipped with multiple *power centers*, each of which plays a role in how you feel, think, and act in any given circumstance and how you feel about yourself and your life, in general. They are: 1) Your emotions; 2) Your intellect; 3) Your spirit; 4) Your physical senses; and, 5) Your intuition. Although you may tend toward leading with one more than another, your power centers are interdependent, and your failure to empower any one of them can inhibit your experience of divine connection and spiritual guidance. Each of the healing practices in this book brings healing to one or more of your power centers, and I invite you to notice which of your power centers is most activated with each practice. You may find yourself being more thoughtful or intuitive, or more emotionally sensitive, or physically active, depending on which of your power centers is being stimulated.

I also invite you to notice when you have a particular resonance with or resistance to any of the practices. "Resonance" means positivity – a feeling of affirmation. When you find a particular practice that resonates with you, celebrate it, dive into it, and expand it. Practice it with devotion and allow the full experience of it to permeate your entire life. When you feel yourself "resisting" or shying away from a practice, take note. Resistance is a sign that one or more emotions have been reactivated by something in the present that reminds you of an unpleasant experience you've had in the past. This reaction is human, but you must remain open to new experiences if you really want to live a powerful life. This book offers you plenty of opportunities to identify the things that activate you and re-activate you. Take this time to learn about yourself, and be open to change. That is how you will bring the energy of healing into your life. That is how you will learn to connect with and expand your "personal power network", if you will.

But, first and foremost, you must be kind to yourself. True healing is a process that isn't always easy. It takes time and intention and often requires us to look inside ourselves in ways that we would rather not. When you feel resistance of any kind – discomfort, fear, anxiety, procrastination, or avoidance – you can be sure that you are entering the land of healing. Do your best to be faithful and take on the practices that appeal to you, no matter how uncomfortable it may be to do so, for it's in the discomfort that true healing takes place. Ultimately it's how you relate to your own healing that's going to make a difference. It's more the *being* than the doing that's going to give you the experience of joy, freedom, abundance, and fulfillment that you are looking for. This book will teach you alternative ways of being that will help you connect more deeply with divine guidance. So, pay attention and be patient. If your intention is to heal, then that is what you will manifest. Having said that, it will be extremely useful for you to create an empowering context for implementing healing practices into your life.

Some questions you might ask yourself are:

- What is missing in my life that would make a difference if it were present?
- What do I intend to accomplish by taking on the practices in this book?
- What do I really want in my life? Who would I like to be? What would I like to do? What would I like to have in my life that could be generated by my taking on these practices?
- How would my life benefit from implementing these healing practices in my life?

Before you move on, I recommend that you take some time to answer these questions for yourself, and any other questions you can think of that will make the lessons in this book more applicable to your life. By choosing to read this book, you have chosen to embark on a journey of self-exploration that will reveal the places in your life that need to be healed in order for you to reclaim your power and set yourself fully on the path to self-actualization. It's time to Heal Your Power and Heal Your Life!

The Healing Practice
of Self-Awareness

Have you ever said something to someone in conversation and then wondered why you said it? Have you ever made a decision that just didn't make any sense? Have you ever missed your exit on the highway or arrived at your destination and realized you were unconscious for part of the trip? We all go unconscious once in a while, right? But, I think you'll agree that it's not the most productive way to live, or the safest, or the healthiest for that matter. What is healthy is being aware of what we are doing, what we are thinking, and how we are feeling at any given moment.

In fact, self-awareness is one of the most valuable practices you can take on. Watching your thoughts, your feelings, your emotions, and your behaviors and noticing how your attitudes and opinions shape your actions is a powerful healing tool. This is because so much of what motivates people is sourced by judgment, fear, insecurity, and reactivated emotions stemming from childhood trauma – all of which occur mostly in the realm of the subconscious. Only by becoming conscious of the connection between your thoughts, your feelings, and your actions can you ever hope to be fully empowered and fully in control of your life.

Those who fail to practice self-awareness are doomed to repeat the past. Nowhere is this more apparent than in the area of self-sabotage – those habitual behaviors that people subconsciously engage in that keep them from moving forward in life. People who sabotage themselves don't allow themselves to take advantage of opportunities. They come up with excuses for why it's not a good time to act on their ideas. They suddenly get sick on the day they are going to a job interview that could skyrocket their career. They make choices that compromise their integrity because they are secretly afraid that life won't work out if they stand up for themselves. These people are mostly unaware of what they're doing or what their motives are.

You may have encountered some self-sabotage in your own life. We all have at one time or another, because we all have experienced some pain in our lives that we don't want to repeat. Whenever people experience trauma of any kind, whether mental, physical, or emotional, the memory of that event is stored in the cells of the body. Cell memory is the reason why so many people report feeling stuck in a cycle of negativity. When traumatic memories occupy valuable space in our energetic bodies and clutter up our spiritual space, they tend to crowd out positive memories. It's not unusual for people to remember "negative" experiences and "negative" emotions far more vividly and for a longer time than those they consider to be positive. You may have experienced this in your own life. If so, you're not alone. Just know that in order to move on, people who feel stuck in this way need to allow negative energy to flow out so positive energy can flow in.

If you find yourself avoiding certain situations all the time, arguing about the same issues repeatedly, or perpetuating the same dysfunctional behavior(s) (whether you are aware of it or not), a repressed memory or stuck energy pattern may be to blame. Unfortunately, these behaviors and thought patterns are barriers to your satisfaction and success, and unless you bring them into your consciousness, you will continue to sabotage yourself. The mistake people make is that they don't realize that these negative behaviors and thought patterns are not who they really are. They're just symptoms of dysfunction. Everyone has experienced some dysfunction in their lives. Just know that the more aware you become of your own dysfunction, the more freedom you will have from your past and the more power you will have in your present. It's that simple, so pay attention to your patterns. If you notice that you are stuck, look closely at the circumstances and see if they remind you of some past experience you never fully recovered from – some painful memory that has resulted in a judgment, an opinion, or a phobia that keeps you from playing full out in your life.

If this is your experience, I suggest you also become more aware of your language. What do you say to yourself? Do you speak kindly to yourself or berate yourself? Do you encourage yourself or do you tell yourself you're not worthy of living a great life? I've devoted a chapter of this book to the healing practice of being self-expressed, which includes, not only how you talk to others, but also how you talk to yourself. Part of being self-aware is noticing your self-talk. When you speak lovingly to yourself, your entire journey becomes one of self-expansion and authentic self-expression.

By expanding your awareness, you expand your capacity, not only for healing your own wounds, but for being a conduit for the healing of others. The more you know about who you are and what you want, the more access you will have to your truest and most authentic self.

So, what stops you from being who you are and having what you want? It's a question I ask all of my clients and potential clients to answer. Why? Because until you know where you stop, you can't move forward. Answers to the "where do you stop" question range from "fear of being embarrassed" to "rudeness in other people".

It's all a matter of what your experiences have been. The problem is that so many people aren't aware of their experiences – not fully, anyway. Instead of tuning into what's happening, it isn't unusual for people to go through life on automatic pilot. The effect of living life this way is a dulling of the senses and a failure to fully tap into the experience of being alive. As children, we are acutely attuned to our experiences – especially our physical experiences. We explore the world with our bodies, and eventually learn to fear certain things – like hot stoves and sharp objects.

While human beings are born with a wide range of emotions, as we grow older, we learn that certain experiences evoke certain emotions, and we learn to avoid those experiences that make us feel uncomfortable. We may avoid interacting with certain people or stop participating in certain activities that we consider to be sources of sadness, frustration, or anger. Over time, we learn to navigate uncomfortable situations by suppressing our emotions. Through social interaction, people learn that in order to survive emotionally (and, in some instances, physically) they must take on behaviors such as lying, pretending to be something they are not, or going along with things they disagree with. Perhaps you've had this experience. In fact, we all have. People need to feel safe! It's just that simple. Sometimes we pretend in order to protect ourselves. There's nothing wrong with protecting ourselves, but when we are protecting ourselves, we need to be aware of that. We need to be aware of when we're pretending, people-pleasing, hiding out, or suppressing ourselves. Then we need to figure out why we're doing that. What are we reacting to? What are we afraid of? What has triggered us to act in such a way?

I was fortunate enough some years ago to be a keynote speaker at a women's conference, where I spoke about the effects of shame and how women react to feelings of shame. One of my favorite authors and transformational gurus is Brene Brown Ph.D., a clinical psychologist who has studied and written extensively on the subject of shame. Dr. Brown is world renowned for her groundbreaking research, which has led her to conclude that shame is a universal experience for women and girls. When I shared my own experiences of shame in that keynote speech, I watched from the stage as one woman after the other began nodding her head in agreement. Some began to tear up. I talk more about shame later in the book, but I bring it up now to make a point. Women are uniquely wired to experience shame because of the way we are socialized, sexualized, and basically made to believe that we aren't as "good", as smart, or as strong as men. The effect this has on us can be devastating to our self-expression. Instead of being authentic, women put on armor to protect ourselves from those shameful feelings. Every time something happens that makes us experience ourselves as "less-than" others, we put on a piece of armor. In my speech, I used sticky notes to make my point. As a child in nursery school, I was part of a Halloween parade. I and the other children in my class paraded around the school, moving from one classroom to the other. At some point I became separated from the class and found myself parading around the classroom alone. I hadn't been able to see through my mask, which was too big for my face, and I hadn't noticed that the other children had moved on to the next classroom. The laughter from the other children signaled to me that something had gone wrong, and I lifted up the side of my mask to see my teacher motioning frantically for me to rejoin the class – unfortunately, not until I had made a fool of myself. For me, this became one of those shameful experiences that lasted a lifetime. The lesson I learned that day was "never stand out".

A year or so before that, my mother had dropped me off at a birthday party in a neighborhood I wasn't familiar with. Most of the kids were older than I was and I didn't know any of them. I still remember standing there in my light blue satin dress with the taffeta slip and patent leather shoes, watching them fight over a toy. When the chaperones finally caught on, everybody got in trouble, including me, an innocent bystander if there ever was one. This is the first time I remember feeling ashamed. At 4 and 5 years old, my suit of armor had already begun to form.

The lesson I learned that day was to never get involved, and to this day, I can't stand crowds and I'm still more of a bystander than a joiner. I could go on. The point is that for most women, the armor building party starts early. This is why self-awareness is so important.

After I left the stage that day, woman after woman came up to thank me for "telling their stories", for helping them see how they had walled themselves in, and for inspiring them to take the armor off and dare to express themselves fully and authentically so they could experience all that life has to offer. Once you develop the ability to see yourself in action and notice when you're hiding behind your armor, you'll have an opportunity to choose whether to keep hiding or let yourself be seen. It will feel risky at first, but the payoff is well worth the discomfort.

Hiding out isn't healthy and it's not the least bit transformative. In order to grow spiritually, we have to be able to access our feelings and express them. When we put on our armor of protection, we think we're hiding from others, but we're really hiding from ourselves. For healing to occur in your life, you need to notice when and why you're suppressing yourself, and what emotions you're avoiding. Allow yourself to become aware of the shame you might be holding onto so you can release it and move on. This process can be difficult, not to mention scary, but must be done in order for you to achieve full spiritual expansion and access your full spiritual and emotional power.

So, it falls on those of us who are committed to standing in our power and living an empowered life to deepen our awareness of who we are, what we do, and what we believe. We need to learn which particular forces in the world take us away from being ourselves, from playing full out in life, and from fully experiencing all that life has to offer. This means being open to experiencing thoughts and emotions that make us uncomfortable. On your journey to enlightenment, you may uncover some things about yourself and your life that you would prefer stay hidden. There may be unfinished business in your past that needs to be addressed – perhaps a relationship that needs to be completed, or a dream that needs to be reawakened and tended to. This is the type of self- exploration that will lead to a greater sense of self- awareness and contribute to the heightened level of emotional intelligence you want and need in order to live a truly empowered life. So, seeing yourself in action and being aware of what turns you on and off, noticing what you react to and how you react to it, knowing what blocks you and what you aren't able to "be with" in life is a critical practice for being the fully empowered "you".

Self-awareness is a healing practice because by noticing where, when, and why you stop playing full out in life you get to see where and how you're letting your past render you powerless in your present. If you don't acknowledge your insecurities and seek out your blind spots, you will continue to avoid situations that make you feel uncomfortable, but that you could actually benefit from if you were able to deal with the discomfort and move forward anyway.

Healing Worksheet – Self-Awareness

Commit to becoming more self-aware. Begin to notice your thoughts, feelings, and actions and how they-relate to each other and to the circumstances of your life. Notice how your thoughts and feelings dictate your actions. Also notice the opinions and judgments you have about yourself and your life. Take note of any repetitive patterns in your life and begin to inquire into where those patterns originated. Notice their effect on your life and inquire into what healing you can bring to that area. Allow yourself the freedom to experience your feelings in any given moment without judgment and with a healthy curiosity about what makes you the uniquely powerful woman you are.

Healing Questions to Promote Self-Awareness

Where am I not playing full out in life?

What are the thoughts and emotions that stop me from playing full out?

What judgments and opinions do I have about myself and my life that keep me from standing in my power?

What are the repetitive patterns in my life?

What are my sabotaging behaviors and where do they manifest most often?

What painful memories need to be healed in order for me to fully stand in my power?

How will my life benefit from fully standing in my power?

Who will I be being? What might I do differently? What might I have that I don't have already?

Which one of my power centers is most activated by this conversation? (Spiritual, emotional, sensual, intellectual, intuitive?)

The Healing Practice of Values Alignment

What are your core values? Do you know? Do you know why you care about some things and not others?

We are all defined and motivated by what we value, and we do well when we live our lives in accordance with those values. But, I bet you can think of at least one time when you allowed someone to talk you into doing something that was not aligned with your values. Perhaps you did something, said something, or pretended to be something that wasn't authentic for you, but that you felt compelled to do at the time. I invite you to recall what that felt like. Do you remember what the consequences were? This type of self-compromise is an everyday occurrence for many women and it's the basis for a good deal of emotional suffering. When we are courageous enough to identify, walk in, and make our core values known, we not only empower ourselves to live authentically, we empower others to do so, as well. All great leaders do this. They stand in their values and invite others to join them. This is what you must do, as well. You must be a leader in your own life.

This requires that you at least be willing to live in accordance with your values, and you may need to assess what your values actually are. To do a "values assessment" make a list of what you like, what you want, what you consider to be important, and what motivates you. Once completed, you may notice that your list is a direct reflection of when and where you grew up, the circumstances of your childhood, who raised you and what their beliefs were. This is square one for each of us. One of the privileges of adulthood (and personal empowerment) is that you can choose newly at any given time. Just because you grew up with a certain set of values does not mean you are obligated to uphold those values for the rest of your life.

"Core values" are traits or qualities that you not only consider to be worthwhile, but that represent your highest priorities, most deeply held beliefs, and fundamental driving forces. Core values are also called "guiding principles" because they form a solid core of who you are, what you believe, and what you want to *be, do,* and *have* in life.

Your core values are also known as your "Why". Why do you do what you do? Why do you care about what you care about? Why do you want what you want? Knowing what you value and why is a critical aspect of self-empowerment; aligning yourself with those values gives you conviction and a commitment to living your life in a way that is pleasing to your spirit. It's very difficult to live with passion if you are not living aligned with your core values. When you compromise on your values, you give away your power and it is important for you to determine where you do that and why. When we compromise on our core values we risk doing harm to ourselves on all levels of our being, in part because this type of compromise is often a result of some negative messages we've allowed to permeate our psyches and affect our better judgment. When we let someone talk us into something we don't want to do, do something we know feels wrong, or bend over backwards to make someone happy, we're reacting to something within us – something that interferes with our ability to stand up for what we believe in. Compromise of this magnitude is also associated with a failure to establish and maintain healthy boundaries.

Healthy boundaries are a critical component of living a powerful life. They help us define ourselves in relationship to others. While healthy boundaries create healthy, functional relationships, unhealthy boundaries create unhealthy, dysfunctional relationships. That's why it's critical that you identify and align with your core values as much as possible.

A key component of loving relationships is the willingness of each partner to be open to including all aspects of the other – all of their spirituality, their intellect, and their physicality, all of their sensibilities, their strengths, and their weaknesses. Being fully ourselves and letting others be fully who they are is critical to nurturing, beneficial relationships. This does not mean that we should let other people take over our lives. When we allow the people in our lives to define us or when we compromise our values for them, we give them all the power and leave ourselves powerless. By the same token, when we attempt to impose our values on the people we love we don't get to know who they truly are. It's easy to assume that we know everything about our partners, but it's a mistake to believe that everything we assume to be true about them actually is the truth. Core values are the essence of what makes us who we are. Where relationships are concerned, especially our most intimate relationships, it is critical that we honor not only our own values, but those of our partners. I have learned this from years of coaching women, and I have experienced it first hand in my own life.

I said earlier that values are subject to change over time, and after 13 years of being married to a wonderfully loving and supportive man, I found that my values had shifted quite dramatically. When we were first married, one of my core values was safety. Marrying my husband provided me with financial stability and with a partner that I trusted to be there for me and treat me well. But, as my spiritual journey progressed, I became more interested in living a fully self-expressed and authentic life and less interested in living a life of safety. I began to crave deep existential conversations about life, love, and the intricacies of the spirit in which my husband was not particularly interested. As someone committed to healing and to helping others heal, it became important for me to be surrounded by people who were also on the path to self-discovery and healing. I wanted more from my relationships. Not only did I want to be able to express my opinions and viewpoints, but I wanted my husband to express his, as well. When no amount of coaxing from me seemed to make a difference, the relationship lost its luster for me. I felt that our relationship had become stagnant. Not only that, I felt that I was suppressing myself in order to avoid disappointment and discord. As a healer and educator in the field of spiritual growth, I felt that it was not acceptable for me to compromise on my values that way – especially with the person with whom I wanted to be most intimate. It was also not appropriate for me to continuously request that he alter his values to fit my needs. It wasn't fair to either of us.

I share this because you may see yourself in this story – in a relationship that was once a source of power for you that now feels like a power drain. This is common, but nonetheless difficult. No doubt, you would want to do a good deal of soul-searching before stepping out of a significant relationship. I know lots of folks who jumped from the frying pan into the fire! If you're feeling dissatisfied in your relationship, you may find that all that is needed between you and your partner is a conversation for new possibilities. Your partner may not know what your core values are. Maybe you've never shared them, or perhaps you're just discovering them for yourself. You might want to have a heart to heart discussion with your partner about what your values are as individuals and as a couple. Maybe you can do a values assessment together and compare. Either way, what is important for you to learn is that when you compromise on your core values, you miss the opportunity to live powerfully and authentically. Unless you know what your values are, you're going to miss a lot of what makes life enjoyable. Shared values make relationships stronger and you owe it to yourself and your partner to do the values assessment exercise. I did this exercise with my husband and it made a tremendous difference in our ability to communicate and compromise in a way that left us both feeling powerful, heard, and appreciated.

One of the practices I recommend to my clients is to do a periodic values alignment check. This practice really comes in handy when you find yourself in a situation where you're feeling uncomfortable or unsure of yourself. It's during those times that you should stop in your tracks, take a deep breath (at least one), put your hand on your heart, and ask yourself what is true for you. Look inside of yourself to determine your best course of action and to ascertain whether your boundaries are being compromised. Alignment checks are empowering, educational, and freeing. Not only can they help you make right choices, but checking in with yourself periodically also builds self-awareness, self-esteem, and the capacity for authentic self-expression.

Living in alignment with your values is a healing practice, because doing so increases your ability and willingness to make right choices, speak your truth, and stand your ground when challenged. Knowing who you are, what you stand for, and why you care about the things you care about creates a powerful context for spiritual enlightenment and divine connection.

Healing Worksheet – Values Alignment

Make a list of your core values. Determine where you are not living in alignment with those values and commit to making the changes necessary to do so. What ways of being do you need to take on or let go of? What lifestyle changes do you need to make? What do you need to say and to whom? How will your life be different when you live your life according to what is really important to you?

<u>Healing Questions to Promote Values Alignment</u>

What are my core values? (What do I care about? What's most important to me?)

Where in my life am I or am I not living in alignment with my core values?

What needs to change in order for me to live in alignment with my core values?

What would be possible for me if I lived in total alignment with my core values?

Who will I be being? What might I do differently? What might I have that I don't have already?

Which one of my power centers is most activated by this conversation? (Spiritual, emotional, sensual, intellectual, intuitive?)

The Healing Practice
of Authentic Living

Authentic living is directly related to the two concepts we just covered, self-awareness and values alignment. Authentic living is about making choices that are right for you, doing what brings you joy, and living in alignment with your divine purpose. Living an authentic life also requires courage and a good deal of intention. If you've ever pretended to be something you're not, played small to make someone else feel comfortable, or stayed too long in situations that weren't right for you, you know what it feels like to be inauthentic. We've all done this from time to time. People do this frequently in situations where they feel uncomfortable being themselves – afraid that what they have to say will not be well-received, or concerned about upsetting the status quo. The unfortunate thing about being inauthentic is that it rarely pays off in the end, and often leaves us dissatisfied and upset with ourselves, the situation, and the people we're in relationship with. In my experience, the ability to live and express oneself authentically is essential to self- empowerment, but not so easily attained.

Being authentic means:

- Being yourself – No faking, pretending, hiding, or holding back
- Telling the truth – Saying what you mean and meaning what you say – No withholding
- Asking for what you want and need – No pretending you have it all together
- Making choices that are right for you – No compromising on your values.

So, who are you, really? It's important for you to know, because only then can you know what is and is not authentic for you. It's not unusual for people to think they're being authentic, when they aren't. This isn't their fault. Sometimes it's because of how they were raised. For most of us, our experiences have taught us that being authentic is not a good thing. Even as children we are told to sit when we want to stand, stand when we want to sit, be silent when we want to speak, work when we want to play, and the list goes on. And the pattern can continue into adulthood – some people experience pressure to become something other than what they might otherwise become – either to make someone else happy or to ensure economic success, etc. It's no wonder that so many people aren't truly happy. People who grow up in environments that do not encourage individuality (and perhaps spontaneity), don't learn the value of being wholly and completely themselves. They may grow up with the belief that they aren't good enough and that being themselves wasn't a good idea or wouldn't get them where they wanted to go in life. People who were raised in this type of environment are typically more likely to sell out on themselves than individuals who grew up in environments that supported individuality and full self-expression. And this is the true meaning of authentic living – being fully self-expressed, being your own person, and living a life of your own design without hesitation or apology.

When your life is a true expression of who you are and what you believe in, you'll find yourself much less worried about how others will receive you. People will choose to interact with you or they won't. Either way, you'll have the satisfaction of knowing that you showed up and you didn't fake it for their sake. Although we've all faked it at some time or another, it's really not helpful, and can be quite harmful. Whenever we misrepresent ourselves in order to gain something we give up our power. For most of us, our first experience with pretending occurs in childhood as a result of peer pressure. For others, it occurs as a result of trying to please our parents or other authority figures. Although all teens experience peer pressure, studies show that adolescent girls put much more pressure on themselves to conform than boys do. In part, this is due to the fact that relationships tend to be more important to girls than to boys, and identities are forged within relationships. For some women, this dynamic remains fairly static, and the pressure to conform to the norms of society takes the place of peer pressure. As archaic as it sounds, women are still asked to choose between career and family and pressured to conform to the ideal images of mother and spouse. Women and girls are bombarded with negative messages about body image and sexuality in the media and are manipulated by retail companies whose goal is to make women buy whatever they think will make them appear younger and more attractive. It is no wonder that so many women find it difficult to share themselves authentically or create lifestyles that are outside of societal norms. This is even more difficult for trauma survivors; whose life experiences provide clear evidence that full self-expression is a dangerous proposition. While my traumatic experiences may not have been as severe as those of others, they were significant enough to make me believe that I was not good enough and that it wasn't safe for me to be myself.

A victim of childhood bullying, I learned to be hypervigilant and distrustful. Because I never told anyone about the bullying - not my teachers nor my parents – I felt fairly abandoned. Instead of standing up for myself, I dealt with it by going further and further inside myself. I chose to protect myself emotionally with my armor of choice. 'You can't hurt me' and 'never let'em see you sweat' became my mantras. With those mantras came life lessons like, 'never stand out', 'never speak up', and 'never fight back'. I was raised to believe that fighting was wrong, and no one ever taught me to stand up for myself in that way, so I didn't. I just absorbed all of that negativity into the fabric of my life. Some years later, at a class reunion, a former teacher complimented me for being "above it all" when I was a student. If she only knew.

Looking back on it now, it all seems so ridiculous. The fact that I let that experience color my life is even more ridiculous, and I would laugh about it, if it weren't so sad. As a result of those years of bullying, I failed to set goals or pursue my passions – art, dance, acting, and psychology. Instead, I let fear dictate my actions and made self-sabotage a favorite pastime. Somewhere along the way I stopped trusting myself to make good decisions, and with good reason. As a child, all I wanted to do was to fit in, and during my teens I made one bad choice after another trying to "get people to accept me". It was many years before I understood that it was self-acceptance I was craving.

Although I had always been an "A" student, I delayed going to college, afraid to make a commitment. When I did finally go to college, instead of majoring in dance, I chose to study liberal arts because it felt less risky. The classes were easy and I graduated with honors. I was even asked to give the commencement address, but feeling I had little to be proud of, I declined the opportunity. Not only did I not speak at my college graduation ceremony. I didn't even attend. The truth is that I was embarrassed that I had not done more with my college career and I did not feel worthy of receiving accolades or congratulations. I have often looked back on those years with regret and self-disdain. How could I have done so little with the opportunities I was given and how could I have failed myself so miserably? Since then I've learned that underachievement and living under the radar are symptoms of low self-esteem, and that self-loathing can be a sign of post-traumatic stress disorder (PTSD) – a result of bullying and other forms of trauma. Now I know that bullying and other acts of aggression are themselves based in fear and have their origins in self-loathing on the part of the aggressors and have absolutely no relationship to the characteristics of the victims. If I had known that when I was a child, I might have made different choices.

My pattern of self-sabotage continued far into my 30's and even 40's and I've had to forgive myself over the years. Instead of finishing my master's degree I moved in with my boyfriend – a mistake that would take me years to get over. Sacrificing myself for men was a pattern that emerged early in my life, and the prospect of getting married (a.k.a. loved and accepted) was enough to make me scuttle a perfectly good graduate career, not to mention a thriving business. I could go on.

Suffice it to say that years of spiritual growth work and a commitment to being self-aware has taught me to understand and accept myself for who I am, to forgive myself for being less than I might have been, and to love myself, regardless. Had I continued down the path of self-sabotage, I may never have written this book, or been able to teach women how to love and honor themselves for who they are, and my life-purpose might have gone unrealized. Last year I finally decided that the emotional baggage of not having finished graduate school was too heavy, and decided to give it another shot. I'm proud to say that I'm earning my master's degree in human behavior. I can't guarantee that I'll graduate with honors, but you can best believe that I *will* attend the graduation ceremony, and I might even dance across the stage!

Living an authentic life is a gift to yourself and to those who know and love you, but there is no shame in failing to be yourself. At some point in our lives, we all pretend to be something we're not. It's one of the ways through which we learn about ourselves. But for us to continually deny our own power is tragic. No degree of self-subjugation could change the fact that I am talented, smart, beautiful, and committed to making an impact in the world. The same is true for you and every woman who is committed to living the life they not only desire, but deserve. Yes, my story is extreme, but it isn't unusual for women to hold themselves back because they are afraid to exert their power. By living an authentic life, you guarantee that your purpose for living will be fulfilled. I like to think that if I had known then what I know now that I would not have wasted so much time. But then, perhaps these are lessons that I needed to learn by experience. If that is so, then I am grateful for them.

So, where are you not living an authentic life? Where have you compromised for safety and security? What would you do, who would you be, and what would you have in your life if you weren't worried about other people's opinions?

Living an authentic life is a healing practice because, by doing so, you honor who you are and what you are here for. The more willing you are to be authentic, the more respect you'll have for yourself and the more you will command the respect of others. I can't overemphasize how important it is for you to be who you really are, say what you really mean, and do what you really want to do. To do anything else would be inauthentic.

Healing Worksheet –
Living an Authentic Life

Begin to notice when you are compromising, hiding, lying, or pretending to be anyone other than your most authentic and powerful self and commit to speaking your truth and standing in your purpose. Commit daily to living your most authentic life by saying what you mean, being who you are, and asking for what you want. Practice standing in your power without apology or explanation. Be the best you that you can possibly be!

Healing Questions to Promote Authentic Living

Where am I not living an authentic life?

Where am I compromising, hiding, lying, or pretending to be someone other than who I truly am?

Where am I not saying what I mean or asking for what I need, desire, or deserve?

Where am I not fully standing in my power?

What can I do to live a more authentic life?

What would be possible for me if I lived a more authentic life?

Who will I be being? What might I do differently? What might I have that I don't have already?

Which one of my power centers is most activated by this conversation? (Spiritual, emotional, sensual, intellectual, intuitive?)

The Healing Practice of Living with Integrity

Integrity is another essential component of living a powerful life. Integrity is much like authenticity, except that it tends to have moral overtones in our society. For the purposes of this book, living with integrity means doing the right thing as you understand it, taking responsibility for your actions, and practicing what you preach. Living with integrity is a way of life that gives you consistency and communicates to others that you can be depended upon to operate at a certain level of accountability. Keeping your word and being on time are examples of behaviors that are consistent with living a life of integrity that so many people seem to overlook. Living a life of integrity has special significance for leaders: executives, pastors, community organizers, government officials, health providers and human service professionals - anyone who is committed to affecting change. If you are called to leadership or are committed in any way to making a lasting impact in your family, community or organization, you'll want to pay special attention to the information contained in this chapter.

The qualities of someone who is living with integrity are:

- Doing what they said they would do when they said they would do it or acknowledging when they have not kept their word.
- Doing what is expected of them and acting in accordance with their position or status.
- Communicating openly without hidden agendas or withholding information.
- Being 100% responsible for any and all results (or lack of results) produced.

If the importance of living with integrity isn't obvious to you, look again. Without integrity there can be no true power. Imagine that you are in a relationship with someone who consistently breaks his or her word to you. After a while, don't you stop trusting that person? That's the way it is for the people in your life with whom you break your word. Even more important, that's the way it is for you when you break your word to yourself! It may not be obvious to you yet, but when you don't keep your promises to yourself, you communicate to your spirit that you can't be trusted and it will be hard for you to sustain any degree of personal power for any length of time. This pattern is best observed when people are out to make a big change in life – perhaps a change in relationships, career, or lifestyle. Large changes such as these require people to step outside of their comfort zones.

This is one of the reasons why people play small in life. When you don't play a big game, you don't make big promises, you don't get out of your own way, and you feel safe. But, when you challenge yourself to step out and play at a higher level, life can get very uncomfortable, which is why it is so important to live with a high degree of integrity. When you live with integrity, you do what you said you would do, often for no other reason than that you gave your word. Following through on your promises keeps you in action. Action breeds confidence and self-respect; inaction breeds complacency and self-contempt. Keeping your word to yourself and others is powerful, breaking your word is not. Living a life of integrity requires that you see yourself in action!

Begin to notice how often you break your word, either to yourself or to someone else. This includes arriving late to appointments, blowing off agreements, fudging on deadlines, and not sticking to an agreed upon regimen. Notice the effect this has on your life, and especially on your relationships. Have you trained the people in your life to expect you to be late, or to break your word? Have they stopped trusting you? Have you stopped trusting yourself? If so, this is a sure sign that the integrity has slipped out of your life and you need to put it back in.

For most of us, this is much easier said than done, but I've never known the effort not to pay off.

Many of my clients are solo entrepreneurs, who come to me because their businesses aren't successful. When they start keeping their word to themselves about making cold calls, going to networking meetings, or whatever it is they need to do but haven't been doing to build their business – that's when the business takes off. I've also worked with managers and executives who have discovered that "do as I say and not what I do" doesn't work when you're counting on people to build your organization. The same can be said for parents who either don't keep their word to their kids, don't set good examples for their kids to follow, or generally don't show up as parents. No matter what your role in life, if you don't show up for the people in your life, you can't expect them to show up for you. If your integrity is out, your reputation is sure to suffer, not only for them, but for you as well.

So, how do you get it back? Again, the quickest and simplest way to do this is to start giving your word and keeping it. Start small and work up. Make promises you know you can depend on yourself to fulfill, and once you have mastered that, start making bigger promises. Nowhere is living with integrity more important than in your relationship with yourself. Being truthful and trustworthy is an act of self-respect. So often people have told me that they manufacture or withhold information because they don't trust people. In reality, not telling the truth signifies a lack of trust in oneself. If you don't believe that who you are is acceptable or good enough, you might be afraid that you won't be able to stand up for yourself when you feel challenged. In some ways that might be true. If you constantly break your commitments to yourself, you have no ground to stand on. When you ask the universe for guidance, you already have an expectation that you won't follow through, which makes your connection with the divine tenuous, at best. If you want the universe to bless you, start keeping your word to yourself and put the integrity back in your life. This is an assignment that I give to all of my clients that many of them find difficult to integrate. The truth is that if you want to have a different life, you will have to do things differently; and that, as they say, ain't easy!

Living a life of integrity is a healing practice because doing so generates positive energy in your life and sets you up to be successful. When you bring integrity to any endeavor, the potential for producing positive results is multiplied exponentially! Living with integrity is more than doing the right thing; it means being responsible for your actions and being willing to be held accountable. As a practice, living with integrity sends consistent messages to you, to the people in your life, and to the universe, that you can be trusted. As you learn to trust yourself, it becomes easier for you to trust that the universe will provide everything you need to live a powerful life.

Healing Worksheet – Living with Integrity

Notice when and how often you break your word, either to yourself or to someone else. Also, take notice of any instances where you aren't being completely truthful, taking responsibility for yourself, or acting in accordance with your agreements. Don't make promises unless you are sure that you are ready, willing, and able to keep them. When you do break your word for any reason, acknowledge it, apologize for it, and make a new commitment if, and only if, you intend to honor it.

Healing Questions to Promote Living with Integrity

Where am I currently not living with integrity?

What effect has that had on my life and on my relationship with myself and others?

What actions can I take to restore my integrity?

Is there anyone to whom I owe an apology or need to make amends?

What would my life be like if I lived with complete integrity?

Who will I be being? What might I do differently? What might I have that I don't have already?

Which one of my power centers is most activated by this conversation? (Spiritual, emotional, sensual, intellectual, intuitive?)

The Healing Practice
of Unconditional Love
and Self-Forgiveness

When you look in the mirror, do you see perfection or fault? Are you someone who tells herself that she is smart, beautiful, loving, and wonderful, or do you constantly judge and criticize yourself? It's not unusual for women to tear themselves down more than they lift themselves up. If I've learned anything over the years, it's that women are their own worst critics. Not only do we judge ourselves more harshly and more frequently than we judge others, but we also don't forgive ourselves as easily as we forgive other people, which sets us up for a lot of unnecessary struggle.

After all, how we think and feel about ourselves creates our environment, our circumstances, and our relationships. When we don't love and acknowledge ourselves for who we are, our perspective becomes skewed; we begin to relate to ourselves as less than worthy and resist our own power. When we believe that we are unworthy, we block our ability to receive love, support, recognition, and abundance of any kind – including money, well-being, and peace of mind. If you want to live a life of abundance, you'll have to transform your feelings about yourself. You'll have to love yourself more, forgive yourself more easily, and resist the urge to judge yourself - and others, as well. Judgment drains your power, forgiveness restores it.

Most women have an abundant supply of emotional baggage they use as evidence for why they don't deserve to be powerful. And, the memories of things they haven't forgiven themselves for or things they haven't forgiven others for make up the majority of that baggage. Memories of this type are fertile ground for self-doubt, self-sabotage, self- criticism, self-loathing, and self-compromise. In other words, when you withhold forgiveness, you not only rob yourself of your power, you set yourself up for suffering by habitually bathing in a pool of reactivated emotions.

It's been said that resentment is like drinking poison and waiting for the other person to die. And, as ridiculous as this sounds, this is exactly what we do when we judge people for how they live their lives or hold onto resentments for how we feel we've been mistreated. Every time we are reminded of that person or the incident associated with that person, we are immediately re-activated. Indeed, we are transported back in time so that the memory of whatever hurt we experienced is once again fresh in our minds, eliciting the exact same physical and emotional sensations. Our heart beat quickens, perhaps we grow angry or tearful or resolve to give that person a piece of our mind when we see them again, even though the hurtful incident may have occurred days, months, or even years ago. And what of the other person? Although he or she may feel sadness or even remorse about having hurt us in some way, they are likely not allowing it to interfere with the living of their lives. This is not always the case, but for the most part, it's true. They've moved on. We're still stewing. Meanwhile, we've cut ourselves off from love, joy, and spiritual abundance by allowing anger, resentment, and who knows what all to build up inside of us, unexpressed and unresolved.

Clients often ask me why they aren't able to experience joy in the moment, self-satisfaction, or peace of mind, and the answer almost always is that they are holding on to hurtful memories and putting so much effort into trying not to repeat the past that they don't allow themselves to enjoy what is right in front of them. I see this, in both men and women, but especially in women. Holding on to emotional baggage is spiritually painful, and hiding the pain makes the baggage heavier. Pain and anger that go unexpressed become lodged in our bodies, wreaking havoc on our emotions until we become spiritually and emotionally stuck. As an empowerment coach, I provide women with a safe space in which to express suppressed emotions like anger, resentment, and shame. When women get in touch with their emotions and express them, they free themselves from the bondage of past hurts and begin the process of healing. When women acknowledge what they've lived through, they can find compassion for themselves, and forgive themselves for whatever wrongs they feel they've done, and they can begin to acknowledge themselves for their accomplishments and create a future that is full of new possibilities.

For one who is unwilling or unable to forgive, joy is fleeting. This is all the more so when the person one is unwilling to forgive is oneself. Harkening back to the analogy of taking poison, I say that refusing to forgive yourself is like taking poison over and over again, trying to kill off old memories that somehow grow sharper with each dose. Guilt, shame, resentment, and anger are emotions that can result from momentary or ongoing trauma, but that can plague us for a lifetime unless we are willing to name those feelings and transform them. The way to transform pain is to treat it with love.

This is why you must do everything you can to create a loving, nonjudgmental environment for yourself, and take time to love and acknowledge yourself for your accomplishments, no matter how small. This means that you have to make yourself a priority in your own life – spend time with yourself and appreciate who you are and what you bring to the world.

From years of coaching women on the subject of forgiveness, I have found that the things women are most ashamed of are not the things we have done, so much as things that have been done to us. If you've been the victim of assault or mistreatment of any kind, I want you to know that none of that was your fault, and you have nothing to be ashamed of. Studies show that women who have been victimized at some time in their lives are the majority, rather than the minority. Shame, therefore, is one of the most prevalent emotions women deal with. What I also know from working with women is that sharing our experiences with each other promotes healing. My experience in workshops bears this out. As soon as one woman begins to share her story, other women in the room nod their heads in recognition, glad to finally know that they are not the only ones living with that particular brand of baggage. The truth is that a woman's journey is fraught with difficulty, and our experiences are more alike than any of us know – that is, until we dare to share our stories. Knowing that we are not alone helps us to be more compassionate and loving with ourselves. Sharing our stories allows us to heal each other, as we allow ourselves to experience the love of our sisters – all of us warriors on the path to forgiveness, freedom, and personal empowerment.

So, to access unconditional love and experience its power, you must first forgive yourself. You must unpack your emotional baggage by identifying the memories that are keeping you stuck and releasing the pain that is holding you hostage. When you fail to forgive others, you cut yourself off from them. When you fail to forgive yourself you cut yourself off from everything. It is impossible to be fully self-expressed, powerful, and authentic in the midst of self-imposed judgment, because judgment works like a censor. When you judge yourself, you not only censor what you put out in the world, you also censor what you let in. If you've been beating yourself up, for any reason at all, you are perpetuating a cycle of negative energy that will greatly hinder your healing process. In order for healing to occur, you'll have to make peace with yourself. I know first-hand the damage that self- judgment can do to a person's spirit. I also know the joy that comes from loving yourself and letting yourself be loved. Even the most ardent of sufferers can recognize that self-imposed suffering makes absolutely no sense. Treat yourself with loving kindness and open your heart to receive the extraordinary gifts that only love can deliver.

So, the question is, what are you holding on to? What's the judgment you have about yourself and your life that does not allow you to experience passion and enthusiasm, to access your gifts, or to fully express your voice in the world? Are you ashamed of your past, afraid that someone will find out that your life was not what you think it should have been?

For a very long time, I was ashamed of myself and ashamed of my life. The choices I made in my teens and early adult life were not only misguided, but had long term consequences. By the time I was 25, I had already sold out on my dreams of being a professional dancer and settled for working in a bank. I had suffered through several emotionally abusive relationships, and instead of taking my leave, had taken it all in stride as if I had somehow brought it on myself. By 35, I had made a decent life for myself, but was haunted by the knowledge that I had settled for less than I really wanted, and was embarrassed to admit that I had allowed my past to keep me from pursuing my dreams. The anger at having been bullied for many years, the regret of not having pursued the career I wanted, the sadness of not having been able to maintain a healthy relationship with a man, and the resentment of knowing that so many of the people around me were happily pursuing their dreams had me completely immobilized. For a long time, I felt dead inside, unable to feel joy, passion, or enthusiasm for anything. Easily bored and even more easily frustrated, I had a lot of trouble completing things. In my mind, I knew I was capable of so much more than I had accomplished, but the embarrassment of having chosen poorly (albeit unconsciously) – of engaging in emotionally abusive relationships, of allowing myself to be bullied, of having turned down so many opportunities to step into the light kept me living under the radar until I finally learned that the only way to have the life I wanted and deserved was to forgive the bullies of my youth, forgive the men who did not love me the way I wanted and needed to be loved, and forgive myself for the choices I had made and how I had lived my life. But, in order to do that, I first had to believe that I was worthy of being forgiven and worthy of living a fulfilling and joyful life.

One of the effects of shame is an intrinsic belief that one is not worthy of being happy, prosperous or, generally speaking, having a good life. This isn't always easy to see, but when I ask people what has them not living the life they want, not pursuing their dreams, or not maintaining healthy relationships, they can see that somewhere along the line they took on the mistaken belief that they were not worthy of experiencing joy and abundance. Of course, I often see it before they do, because I lived it for so long and I recognize the signs and symptoms associated with this type of disempowerment. My experiences have made me wise in this area, and you would do well to recognize that the experiences of your life are a great source of wisdom, not only for you, but for the people who come to you for healing and strength. I'll always remember with fondness one of my coaches who, having heard me rattle off a long string of complaints about what I hadn't accomplished and where I had failed, calmly suggested that I might want to put down the stick. When I asked her what stick, she just as calmly responded, "the stick you're using to hit yourself over the head". I thought that was hilarious, but I completely got the point, and I've never forgotten it.

The truth is that we have all been created with a divine purpose and an abundance of gifts to share with others. That anyone should believe that she is somehow unworthy of living a fabulously abundant life is tragic.

Every time I conduct a healing workshop, women share how past experiences have kept them from being fully self-expressed – how fear of not being good enough has held them back from being, doing, and having what they really want, and how the shame associated with past trauma has kept them from acknowledging their gifts and stepping into their calling. I consider myself extremely fortunate to be present when those women discover that who they are is not the sum total of their experiences, but divinely gifted by God, having survived some horrific circumstances, and therefore given the purpose of helping others weather similar circumstances to emerge victorious.

If you're a mom, this has special significance. Mothers are responsible for teaching their children how to love and be loved, and daughters are especially sensitive to these messages. It isn't unusual for mothers to inadvertently pass on their shame to their daughters. Indeed, shame is often passed down through generations.

Often it's the people we care about the most that we judge most harshly, and we must be cognizant of that fact, especially when it comes to our children.

For the most part, daughters learn self-worth from their mothers, and as mothers, we owe it to our daughters to do everything we can to make sure they develop into strong, self-aware, self-motivated women who love themselves no matter what. In order to do that, we have to watch what we say not only to them, but to ourselves. Girls are painfully intuitive when it comes to their mothers. They can feel what we're feeling and they tend to internalize our judgment of them (and of ourselves).

Today, more than ever, girls need people they can rely on to breathe positivity into their lives and help them to love and accept themselves for exactly who they are. In order to be all that our daughters need us to be, we need to be for ourselves – to love ourselves, to forgive ourselves, and to be open and transparent with our daughters. Sharing your story with your daughter at the right time can potentially create a bond between the two of you and help her understand that she is not alone in her journey. She'll also know that she can count on you for unconditional love and support, which is critical for her self-esteem and her ability to make empowered choices.

Practicing unconditional love and forgiveness is a healing practice because it instantly transforms all negative energy and allows the energy of abundance to flow into your life without effort. By creating the context for love and forgiveness in your life, you create new avenues for self-expression and new opportunities for prosperity. By treating yourself lovingly, you open your heart to receiving abundance in all of its forms. You open your mind to new possibilities and free yourself up to be the loving and powerful person you were always meant to be.

So – love yourself, forgive yourself, and let yourself be healed! Make it a point to send yourself loving messages. Tell yourself that you are beautiful, smart, talented, and wonderfully made (even if you don't yet believe it). I am living proof that doing this makes a difference! Stand in the mirror and smile at yourself, admire your beautiful body and your indomitable spirit. Acknowledge yourself for anything and everything. Nothing is too small! When someone gives you a compliment, say thank you and stop there. Make a habit of doing this on a regular basis and watch the magic happen!

Healing Worksheet – Unconditional Love and Self-Forgiveness

Visualizations – In the tradition of many healing rituals, I often use water as a source of symbolic purification when I teach healing workshops. I might invite the women in my classes to imagine that they are washing themselves in the sea of forgiveness – purifying their minds and bodies, and freeing their spirits from the tyrannical binds of shame and regret. You might also think of forgiveness as the river that must be crossed in order to get from the shores of self-limitation to the shores of joy, freedom, and spiritual prosperity. You can imagine yourself wading across the river of forgiveness, crossing from the shore of anger to the shore of unconditional love, and as you do, allowing the water to wash away sadness, emptiness, dissatisfaction, and whatever else has taken over your life.

Journaling – Write about your experiences. What happened? How did it feel? What about that experience are you holding on to? What have you made that experience mean about you? What have you been holding on to that you can now let go of? What can you now forgive yourself for? What can you forgive others for?

Mirror work – Spend time *being* with yourself in the mirror. Say "I Love You" to yourself. Tell yourself that you are beautiful, smart, talented, and wonderfully made. Make a habit of doing this on a regular basis and watch the magic happen!

Affirmations – Write down some affirmations and post them someplace where you will be able to see them. For optimal results, read them every day – out loud, if possible. Reciting your affirmations daily will create the positive energy you need to generate love and forgiveness in your life.

Some possible affirmations might be: I forgive myself for... I forgive (person's name here) for... I give myself the gift of forgiveness... I love myself unconditionally... I am worthy of receiving love... I am open to receiving love and compassion... I acknowledge myself for...

Healing Questions to Promote Unconditional Love and Self-Forgiveness

What painful memories am I holding on to?

How has holding on to these memories affected my life?

What have I not forgiven others for? What would be possible if I forgave that person?

What have I not forgiven myself for? What would be possible if I forgave myself?

Where am I not treating myself with love and compassion?

What can I do to treat myself with more love and compassion?

How would my life benefit from treating myself with more love and compassion?

Who will I be being? What might I do differently? What might I have that I don't have already?

Which one of my power centers is most activated by this conversation? (Spiritual, emotional, sensual, intellectual, intuitive?)

The Healing Practice of Kindness and Generosity

When you say the word "generosity", what comes to mind? Does it bring up images of giving your time and/or possessions to others? You've likely seen the bumper sticker that advises you to practice "random acts of kindness", urging you to be a force for good in the world. But, did you ever consider that being kind and generous not only refers to what you can do for others, but also to what you can do for yourself? The truth is that generosity is a two-way street. When you give, you also receive. And, while it's true that being kind to others does support the flow of positive energy, being kind to yourself is an equally powerful practice.

It isn't unusual for women to give of themselves. Generosity is in our makeup. But, while we know that giving to others is a virtue and creates good energy, we often forget to include ourselves in the formula.

We give, and give, and give. But, receiving? That's a problem for us. Over time, this cycle of giving without receiving can lead to disappointment, resentment, and even anger. Receiving grace from others is a part of our spiritual purpose, and when we cut ourselves off from receiving, we take ourselves out of the natural flow of life. As we've seen in previous chapters, the opposite of flow is resistance, and resistance leads to stagnation.

The important thing to remember is that abundance is universal. God means for us to be both givers and receivers. Part of our mission as human beings is to show kindness and give assistance to other human beings. As spiritual beings, it's part of our purpose to be vessels through which goodness can flow. It is, therefore, inauthentic for anyone to claim that they would rather give than receive, or that they don't have a problem with being alone (all the time). Human beings are not meant to be solitary. In addition, there are people in the world that we are meant to help. Consider the possibility that for every person on the planet, there is at least one other person (in reality there are many more than that) to whom you are divinely contracted to offer some type of assistance. Consider, also, that there are just as many people who are contracted to offer assistance to you! What do you think being at the right place at the right time is all about? Think back to a time when you met someone who gifted you with something useful and you thought you had just gotten lucky. Was that luck, or is it possible that both the meeting and the gift were preordained? Another thing I'd like you to consider is that whenever you allow someone to contribute to you, that you also give them a gift in return. Think of the last time you gave someone a gift or helped them in some way. Did you not feel contributed to? It's in our nature to give *and* receive grace. But we have to allow ourselves to do so.

Life can be difficult, and it often teaches us that giving of ourselves or receiving gifts from others isn't safe. This is an issue of trust. Either we don't trust that what we have to offer has value, and therefore don't offer it, or we don't trust that we ourselves are worthy of receiving grace, and we refuse to accept the gifts that are there for us. I've seen this manifest in many ways.

Some people find it difficult to maintain healthy, loving relationships or engage in co-dependent relationships. Others feel stuck in careers that no longer serve them or bounce from job to job with no sense of satisfaction. Still, others fail to request adequate compensation for their services or live above their means. For trauma survivors or people who have severe trust issues, this is especially common. I've encountered many powerful women, especially women of color, who fall into one or more of these categories. For a while, I was one of them.

The characteristics of "strength" and "sacrifice" have long been a part of Western society's stereotypical image of women. In the case of African-American women, for whom these stereotypes are woven into generations of black culture, this presents even more of an issue. In my opinion, being strong in the face of adversity and being willing to sacrifice for the good of others are just two of the attributes that work both for and against black women. As a black woman, I have no fear in saying these things. Neither do I hesitate in saying that the "strength-sacrifice" stereotype affects not only black women, but all women; it seems that, for some reason, women are expected to do more with less. This is evidenced in the workplace, where women earn far less than their male counterparts. Often, women will collaborate and share the credit for a job well-done, but fail to request compensation for their own hard work. Again, willingness to collaborate is an attribute that clearly works for women in many cases, but a woman's willingness to place the needs of another over her own must be closely monitored. Compromise is one thing, sacrifice is another.

My point here is that subjugation of women in Western society is insidious, and we are paying the price for having subconsciously bought into the idea that women are somehow worth less than men. While this is not the only source of false information that might prevent a woman from being open to fully receiving, it is a huge factor that, despite anti-discrimination laws, has not changed much over the years. For women of color, LGBT individuals, and women with disabilities and other stigmatizing conditions there is even more negativity to overcome. The first step in doing so is to treat yourself with kindness, to be your biggest champion, and to be generous with yourself whenever possible. That does not mean buy yourself gifts that are not supported by your income. It means give yourself the love and respect you deserve, and open your heart to receiving that love and respect from others. Stand for being fairly compensated. Give of yourself when appropriate, but not to the point of sacrifice, and allow yourself to receive the abundance that is your birthright. The universal law of attraction tells us that those who ask for what they need and what they want get it far more often than those who don't. Stand in your value and honor your strengths and abilities. You may get less than you ask for, but you will surely get more than if you had not asked at all. The universe responds to those who stand up for themselves, those who speak their truth, and those who step out into the open.

One of the illustrations I often use with clients is that of a woman who has a child who wants to be recognized for some achievement, or just loved for who he or she is. Imagine that you are the mother in this scenario, and your child is asking for attention at a time when you are busily attending to something else, and you are unable to give her what she needs in the moment. How would you handle this situation? Would you scream at your child or would you speak lovingly to her – letting her know that you will attend to her needs when your task is complete? Hopefully, you would choose the second option, yes? In the normal scheme of things, would you not encourage your child to be proud of her accomplishments? And, what about mistakes? Would you punish her for being human or would you help her to understand that mistakes are to be expected and that she shouldn't beat herself up when she makes one? I suspect that most women would of course agree that this plan of action is completely appropriate, but they would not come to that conclusion when the mistakes are their own. Instead of seeking out or even allowing themselves to be recognized or contributed to, some women treat themselves as if they're unworthy – something they would never do to someone else. If this is a familiar scenario, take heed. If you are treating yourself harshly for mistakes you made long ago and for which you haven't forgiven yourself, then what is called for here is compassion, not punishment. Treat yourself as you would a precious child in your care – love her, be generous with her, and treat her with kindness, for she is worthy of receiving love in all its forms.

When you treat yourself with kindness, you increase your capacity to treat others with kindness. When you are generous with yourself, you can better accept the generosity of others. When you can show up for yourself as worthy, you give yourself the space to be who you really are and afford others the same opportunity. By being generous with your space, your knowledge, your love, and your spirit, you not only show up as a powerful force for prosperity and goodness in the world, you open yourself to receive prosperity and goodness, as well. When you withhold yourself for whatever reason – whether it be fear, doubt, or scarcity you cut yourself off from the flow of abundance. More importantly, however, you cut yourself off from the flow of love.

When you give and receive freely, you give the universe permission to bestow its gifts upon you. In that way, receiving is an act of generosity, both for yourself and for the universe. The ability to give and receive is the basis for intimacy, and relationships thrive when both parties are willing and able to give and receive freely. When you are open to receiving freely, you are better able to access your divine gifts and the career you deserve can flow to you more easily. When you are willing to give of yourself and allow others to give to you, you will achieve greater financial prosperity. We've already discussed the benefits of self-love and self-forgiveness. Being kind and generous with yourself is just as important and the results in your life will be just as powerful.

Practicing kindness and generosity is a healing practice because when you are generous with yourself and treat yourself with loving kindness you elevate your sense of self-worth, empower your self-expression, and exponentially increase the amount of positive energy that flows into and emanates from your life. When you contribute to others and allow yourself to be contributed to, you not only serve your God-given purpose, you expand your spiritual and emotional capacity to live a fully empowered life.

Healing Worksheet – Kindness and Generosity

Are you blocking your blessings? Begin to observe yourself in action concerning abundance. Notice your relationship with giving and receiving. Create a daily practice for opening your heart to receive all blessings from the universe – including money, compliments, assistance, and support. Perhaps practice some affirmations: I am open to receiving abundance in all its forms… I deserve to be recognized for… I am worthy of receiving God's blessings…

Healing Questions to Promote Kindness and Generosity

Where am I not treating myself with loving kindness?

Where am I not being generous with myself?

How do I feel about receiving recognition? Do I seek it out/accept it/avoid it/reject it?

Do I receive compliments gracefully?

Do I feel worthy/unworthy of receiving abundance? Am I blocking my own blessings?

What actions can I take to treat myself more kindly and bring more abundance into my life?

How will my life be affected by treating myself with more kindness and generosity?

Who will I be being? What might I do differently? What might I have that I don't have already?

Which one of my power centers is most activated by this conversation? (Spiritual, emotional, sensual, intellectual, intuitive?)

The Healing Practice
of Gratitude

To get the most out of this chapter, think back to what you learned in the chapter about unconditional love. Recall that opening your heart to receiving love increases the flow of love into your life and that resisting love, or feeling that you are unworthy of receiving love, will likely cause struggle and resentment. Gratitude is much like unconditional love; practicing gratitude means letting go of resistance and struggle so that love and abundance can flow in.

Just as fear attracts fear and love attracts love, being able to express gratitude for the circumstances of your life will bring you into a state of amazing positivity and unadulterated grace. Of course, I am sure that there are many circumstances and situations in your life that you would rather not have to deal with, and you might be wondering how you can be grateful for those particular things. But, it is possible. To be clear, in this instance, the term gratitude refers to your *acceptance* of things the way they are. You don't have to like or condone something or someone in order to be grateful for that thing or that person. Adopting an *Attitude of Gratitude* is about adjusting your focus. Often people try to change their lives by focusing on what they don't like in order to generate something different. However, if what you focus on is what you don't want or don't like, you are sure to invite more of it into your life. When we can be grateful for what "is", our relationship with reality is strengthened and enhanced. When we meet reality without struggle, we can stop wishing things were different and we can focus on being present to the beauty and wonder of life as it is.

Think of the unpleasant situations in your life and identify the thoughts and feelings that have surrounded those situations. Has there been upset, for instance? Regret? Pain? Anger? What if you could change all of that just by adopting "an attitude of gratitude"? What if by accepting things the way they are (even if you don't like them), you could, not only transform your current circumstances, but also pave the way for your future circumstances to be positive and abundant? What if accepting things the way they are could actually transform your relationship to your life from one of struggle to one of pain-free living? What if accepting things the way they are could transform your relationship to yourself from one of limitation to one of freedom and empowerment? When you practice gratitude, not only will you attract the things that you desire in life, you will also begin to experience yourself as powerful, flexible, and free. By practicing gratitude, you not only disappear the experience of lack, you also create the context for abundance to flow into your life.

Gratitude is about feeling and expressing appreciation for all that we have and all that we will ever have. It is also about expressing appreciation for all of our experiences (the good and the bad). What there is to understand here is that nearly all experiences have both positive and negative aspects to them, and if we think about it, there is always something to be grateful for, no matter the circumstances. The wonderful thing about gratitude is that it helps us to shift perspective away from those things that annoy us or seem to stand in the way of our happiness, and shift us toward contentment and peace of mind. Through an experience of gratitude, we can access spiritual understanding and appreciation for why things are the way they are, and expand our ability to live life gracefully, rather than struggle against it at every opportunity. I don't know about you, but in my book, grace beats struggle every time!

One of the most amazing things about gratitude is its effect on well-being. People who practice gratitude on a daily basis experience better physical and psychological well-being, are better able to cope with adversity, and have stronger relationships. For individuals who struggle with anger, resentment, and self-judgment, a gratitude practice helps to dissipate negative energy and facilitates change management. Not that our lives will ever be all "good", but adopting a gratitude practice helps to increase the flow of "good" energy both biologically and energetically, and helps us to experience life as a pleasurable experience, regardless of our circumstances. I'm always astounded and humbled when I meet people who are willing to practice an attitude of gratitude in the direst of circumstances, including homelessness, unemployment, illness, and tragedy. I am amazed by the resilience of the human spirit and humbled by those who have endured far more than I ever have, and yet, continue to be grateful in spite of their circumstances. And, while being aware of the suffering of others is sobering, practicing gratitude is about more than that. Practicing gratitude is about transforming your relationship to your own experiences in a way that frees you up to be all of who you are at every given moment.

Instead of complaining about your job or your car, for example, practice being grateful that you have those things. If you don't like something about yourself, your appearance, your voice, or your hair, perhaps, being grateful for those things puts it all in perspective as you realize how fortunate you are to have a body, a voice, and a full head of hair. It's uncanny how much time and energy human beings spend complaining about their lives – time and energy that could be better spent appreciating and enjoying life and making a difference for one another.

Even as a woman in my 40's, I struggled to understand the experiences and circumstances of my life. While it was easy for me to be grateful for my middle-class upbringing and generally good financial situation, I felt a good deal of anger and resentment toward the people who had hurt and disappointed me. I was also angry at myself for the bad choices I had made, for the opportunities I had missed, and for the way I had summarily handed my power over to fear and let one dream after the other go by the wayside. Adopting a gratitude practice helped me shift my perspective. By entertaining the idea that I could actually be grateful for each and every one of my experiences, even those that caused me pain, I was able to access compassion and forgiveness, both for myself and for those people whom I felt had wronged me. Instead of framing my experiences as wasted opportunities, I was able to see them as learning opportunities. At some point I came to understand that the lessons I learned were valuable, not just for me, but for other women and girls, and I needed to share them. In this way, I was able to transform the anger and resentment that had kept me stuck for so many years into creative energy that helped me launch my coaching practice and write my first book – *Be Your Biggest Champion – A Self-Esteem Guide for Teen Girls*. When I was able to see what my life had produced, it made it easier to leave the pain behind and get present to other possibilities.

Since then, I've shared the power of gratitude with clients and women's groups, and the results are always the same. Women report a greater sense of freedom, love, self-acceptance, and grace. When you accept what's so and express gratitude for what life has given you, your experience of life transforms. For people who struggle with self-acceptance and forgiveness, a gratitude practice helps them to see the purpose of their life experiences and to bring meaning and perspective to their lives. Once freed of struggle and regret, people who have experienced hardship can apply their experiences to make an impact in the world, rather than be swallowed up by them. In other words, they turn their madness into their ministry. There is no shortage of trial to triumph stories in the world. When you're grateful for all you have, you can learn from your trials and appreciate the power you've earned from the lessons you've learned! Practicing gratitude has made me a better coach and author because I can embrace my experiences and use them to enhance my ability to support people. Because I have a greater sense of well-being, I can be more present with my clients – I spend less energy worrying and more energy making a difference.

Gratitude is a daily practice – and it does take *practice*. Unfortunately, we do not live in a world that is geared toward being grateful or generous. Rather, the world we live in is contentious, competitive, greedy, and a constant reminder to people of what they don't have. Being grateful for what you have and what you don't have, who you are and who you are not, and being compassionate with yourself and others creates an atmosphere of love, abundance, joy, and freedom of choice.

Practicing gratitude is a healing practice because when you elevate acceptance you minimize struggle, you deal in reality rather than fantasy, and you can be more of who you are instead of struggling to be who you *think* you need to be to make up for what you *think* you lack. Notice, the emphasis here on the word "think", and remember that it is only our thoughts that truly limit us. Practicing gratitude will not only help you accept yourself and your life, it will support you on your journey to healing and self-empowerment. You were born for greatness. Be careful not to give more attention to challenges than they deserve. Challenges are only challenges if we say they are. When we can generate appreciation for the challenges as well as the successes, we find that we can do more, be more and have more of the best things in life.

Healing Worksheet – Gratitude

Create a daily gratitude list. Each morning and/or evening list 1-5 things that you are grateful for. You can even be grateful for things that haven't happened yet. There are no rules. This is a practice to increase positive healing vibration, and it works. So, just do it! "I am grateful for…"

Write a gratitude letter to someone in your life to express appreciation for ways they may have helped you or been there for you along the way. You can write to thank them for something in the past or something that is occurring in the present. A gratitude letter is a good way to heal a relationship at those times when you are feeling at odds with someone in your life.

Healing Questions to Promote Gratitude

What are the experiences and who are the people that I am most grateful for?

What lessons have I learned from those people and experiences?

How have those lessons affected my life and what about them can I be grateful for?

What actions can I take to generate an attitude of gratitude?

How can walking in gratitude benefit my life?

Who will I be being? What might I do differently?
What might I have that I don't have already?

Which one of my power centers is most activated
by this conversation? (Spiritual, emotional, sensual,
intellectual, intuitive?)

The Healing Practice of Intuitive Listening

Intuition is the ability to know something in the absence of physical evidence. It's my experience that all women have a fairly advanced sense of intuition, but many of us don't use it to our advantage, if at all. Instead of searching our hearts for the answers we seek, we often look outside of ourselves. But, most of the time, if we are willing to be honest with ourselves, we already know the path we should follow. The heart always knows, we just need to be quiet enough and courageous enough to hear it and follow its direction. Think of your intuition like a compass that you can use to locate your "true north". Not only is your intuition an expression of your inner wisdom, but it's also connected to "divine wisdom". To access it, you have to be willing to stop thinking so much with your head (which is the birthplace of fear) and start thinking with your heart (which is the birthplace of love).

No doubt you have heard the phrase, "Follow your bliss" or "Follow your heart". The reason those phrases exist is because the answer to life's problems and the secret to unlocking the doors to happiness and abundance lie in the heart space. Your heart is where you will find your passion, your purpose, and your sense of well-being. The problem is that society sends us so many false messages about who we need to be and what we need to do to compete in life that the messages of our hearts can easily get drowned out. Thinking with your heart and not your head can be risky and extremely scary, but that is what you must do in order to grow, to connect with your spiritual power, and to live a life of joy and emotional freedom.

Often, people find themselves trying to figure out which direction to go and what choices to make, getting caught up in a cycle of self-doubt, fear, and judgment. When you find yourself in this place, tapping into your intuition is a tool you can use to determine what is most authentic for you; it's one of the things that connects you with your divine essence. Some people talk about receiving "intuitive hits" – a gut feeling about how to proceed or a premonition of what is about to occur. These intuitive hits are messages from the universe offering instruction about the steps we should take to access our destiny and move through life with ease and grace. When you allow fear and self- doubt to displace your intuition, you have effectively disconnected from divine guidance. Over the years, I've learned that it's a mistake to question intuition. When you question your intuition, you delay your destiny, cut yourself off from love, and stand in the way of your joy. If intuitive hits are messages from your higher power, what sense does it make to argue?

How many times have you not followed through on an idea for a business or some other idea you had for moving your life forward and lived to regret it? Conversely, how often has your gut told you not to take a particular action and you've realized later that had you heeded your own advice, it wouldn't have been quite so costly? My Achilles heel has been relationships. From trial and error, I've learned that my first instinct about people is usually the right one. My clients experience the same thing, and I hope that you will remember to apply this lesson in your own life, if you have not done so already. Poet Laureate Emeritus Maya Angelou is quoted as saying, "When people show you who they are, believe them." I couldn't agree more. I don't know how many women I've met in my workshops who are generous enough to share their stories of being stuck in relationships that no longer serve them and of taking care of the needs of others while putting their own needs on the back burner. In these encounters I've had the privilege of teaching women how to tap into their intuitive listening. The truth is that, in our hearts, we know whether or not what we are doing serves us. Whether or not we listen to our intuition is mostly a function of self- esteem and our ability to muster the courage to step away from the familiar and venture into the light.

As someone who has struggled for years with self-doubt, it has taken me a great deal of time to trust my own intuitive abilities. Sometimes the consequences of not obeying my intuition have been severe, other times not so much. But, whenever I have listened, the results have always been spectacular. I could tell you that learning to trust your intuition is easy, but I'd be lying. What I can say is that learning to trust yourself is a gift and it's totally worth the risk of being wrong now and then. The more you practice listening with your heart, the more reliable your intuitive sense will become. All it takes is patience and a willingness to get out of your head; intuitive guidance is a heart- based operation.

Think of it this way. Imagine that your head and your heart are opposing radio stations. Mostly people spend way too much time listening to the "head station", which is very, very, loud! The "head station" airs shows like "Voices of Reason" and "Shoulda, Woulda, Coulda". What we need to do is tune into the heart station and turn the volume up because the heart channel is much more peaceful and much quieter than the noisy head station! The "heart station" airs shows called "You Are Good Enough" and "Don't Worry, Be Happy". When you think of it this way, you can begin to get a sense of how different your heart and head messages are, and the urgency with which you need to tune into your heart.

An easy way to do that is to spend a few minutes each day tuning into your intuition by asking your heart to reveal to you the answers you are searching for. There is no limit to the information that your intuition can reveal to you. But, you do need to ask, you do need to listen, and you do need to stop looking outside of yourself for the answers. They're already there in your heart.

Ultimately, failure to listen to your intuition has emotional and spiritual consequences. When you continue to make choices with your head rather than your heart, you make yourself more vulnerable to outside influences that may not be in alignment with your nature or your purpose. Now, I suspect that if you're reading this book, you've decided to take a more spiritual path in your life. If that is true, you will also need to make a commitment to both hear and heed the voice of your spirit when it tells you what to do, where to go, and how to show up in your life. Failure to do so will only result in what I call "spiritual constipation" – clouded thinking, false starts, and an inability to make decisions.

I remember watching a game show at the gym while I was walking on the treadmill. I don't generally watch game shows, but I recall being excited because the contestant, who happened to be an African American woman, was on a roll. Her task was to guess the price of a car. One by one, she had guessed each number in the price correctly, without help from her friends or from the audience, who by that time were going berserk. But, with one more number to go, she turned and asked the audience for help. I can only imagine her disappointment when her final guess was incorrect. She had trusted her intuition to get her almost to the end of the contest, and blew it by asking the audience to weigh in. Unfortunately, I've seen this scenario play out in many different ways in my own life and in the lives of those I know and love. Rather than trusting our intuition to lead us in the right direction, we've blown it by looking outside ourselves for the answers, failing to understand that divine guidance is available to us whenever we listen to our own hearts.

Spiritual guidance is available to everyone. To access it you need only ask for it and be willing to receive it, but to benefit from it you need to actually follow it. The best advice means nothing if not taken. So it is with spiritual guidance. You can pray all day long for guidance, but if you don't follow it because you don't agree with it or because it doesn't fit your picture, you won't receive the blessings that are associated with that guidance. One of the benefits of spiritual guidance is that it will help you discover your true self and step into your divine purpose. Once you see who you are, it's important that you actually be who you are; denying your true self is painful. You are magnificent, special, gifted, and worthy of having absolutely everything life has to offer. When you accept and align with that fact, you not only honor yourself, you also honor God by acknowledging, accepting, and walking in the purpose that was designed specifically for you. If that is what you want, then developing your intuitive abilities is a must!

Tuning into your intuition is a healing practice because your intuition is your pathway to truth, and tuning into it can help you sift through any false and disempowering messages you may be receiving in the present or perpetuating from your past. If you trust it, your intuition will guide you to the relationships, circumstances, and opportunities that will move you toward your highest good and help you discern right choices for your life.

Healing Worksheet – Intuitive Listening

Begin a daily practice of checking in with your intuition. One way you can amplify your intuitive voice is to close your eyes, place your hand on your heart, and breathe very deeply and slowly, while you ask yourself these questions: What do I need today? What will serve my highest good? Remember that intuitive hits are messages from the divine. Have your "ear out" for those divine messages and follow their instructions. You can trust that they will lead you in the direction of your spirit.

<u>Healing Questions to Promote Intuitive Listening</u>

What is my relationship with my intuition? Connected/Disconnected?

When have I listened to my intuition? When have I not listened to my intuition?

How would my life benefit from receiving more divine guidance?

What can I do to have more divine guidance in my life?

Who will I be being? What might I do differently? What might I have that I don't have already?

Which one of my power centers is most activated by this conversation? (Spiritual, emotional, sensual, intellectual, intuitive?)

The Healing Practice of Choosing Consciously

Has there ever been a time in your life when you felt you had no choice or that the circumstances of your life were out of your control? This is a common feeling for many people, and one of the reasons people give up the search for fulfillment. A life without choices would be dull, indeed, and it can be hard to keep a positive attitude when you feel that what happens in your life is out of your control. But, is your life ever really out of your control and are you ever really without choices? The answer is, no, not really. Although it may not always seem like it, you always have a choice. It may not be the choice you want, but you always have one. The hard part is learning to recognize choices for what they are and making a choice that makes us feel empowered rather than defeated.

In my experience, people have several reactions when it comes to making choices. They choose consciously, or they choose unconsciously. People who choose consciously reap the benefits of their choices. People who choose unconsciously forfeit the opportunity to control their circumstances. Too often people give their power away to their circumstances, feeling that they don't have any other choice. Or, they get so overwhelmed with the number of choices that are available to them that they simply throw up their hands in disgust. What's similar about both of these scenarios is the failure to make a choice – the failure to stand in one's power – the failure to embrace the opportunities that life presents us with every day. What these people may not know is that the act of "not choosing" is a choice in itself. One can choose consciously or unconsciously, but one can never "not choose".

Picture yourself at a crossroads with a decision to make. Now imagine that you are free to choose to go in either direction, knowing that down either path lies the unknown. For many people, facing the unknown is enough to keep them standing at the crossroads for quite some time. Afraid of making the wrong choice, many people opt to remain stagnant in what is known, even when the known is miserable for them. Have you had that experience? I know I have. Trusting my intuition has been a struggle for me, and making choices has been extremely difficult. What I've come to realize, however, is that whether I ventured down the path or decided to stay at the crossroads, I had chosen. I may not have chosen powerfully (or consciously), but I had chosen, nonetheless.

The fact is that life itself is a series of choices, and people do well to realize that fact and embrace the choices as they come. But, often they are hard to recognize. From the time we choose to get up in the morning until the time we choose to retire at night, we are presented with opportunities to lead or be led, to be joyful or complain, to create something new or observe the status quo. Everything, absolutely everything, is a choice. And, we do ourselves a disservice when we allow ourselves to be at the mercy of whatever happens along the road of life instead of taking the wheel.

Sometimes there really is just one choice available to us. It's at those times that choosing consciously is the most empowering, because when we choose our circumstances, whatever they are, we choose reality. We don't waste time wishing that life were different, which takes us completely out of reality. Have you ever had the experience of your body being one place but your mind being someplace else? Have you noticed that life just keeps on going, whether you're present for it or not? While you're wishing for things to be different, you may be missing opportunities that are available to you in the present. That's why it's important for you to choose your life – consciously!

It's no fun standing at the crossroads, wishing you could make a choice. And, it's no fun when life chooses for you and gives you less than you might have had if you had chosen for yourself. When you choose what's in front of you, you can embrace reality and enjoy whatever is there. When you don't choose reality, your spirit will surely suffer.

When I learned this fact it changed my life, because it was then that I realized I didn't have to suffer through life the way I had been doing. In fact, I know now that suffering, like everything else, is a choice. One can choose to embrace life, with all its ups and downs, or one can choose to suffer. One can choose to live powerfully and with conviction or choose to be wishy washy and irresolute. People can choose to be at odds in their relationships, or choose to remain calm and centered even in the face of disagreement. It's just that simple. And, although this concept may be hard to grasp, it is important that you map it onto your life and consider the difference it will make in your ability to live powerfully and authentically when you consciously choose how life occurs for you. Empowerment is a choice, and so is "stuck". Again, it's all in how you think about it.

I have a scenario I like to use with clients when they're feeling stuck and unable to choose. I ask them to picture themselves sitting on a fence with arms outstretched in both directions, unable to move in either. I ask them to imagine the physical discomfort of sitting atop a fence with arms outstretched for long periods of time and I invite them to consider the consequences of such an act – the pain of being on that fence, the stress of being out in the elements, unable to eat or sleep. And then I ask them to map the visualization onto their lives. The emotional and spiritual stress one endures during periods of indecisiveness is similar to the physical pain one might experience sitting on an actual fence. Can you imagine the cost of such an act? Indecision is painful. Choosing consciously is the only way to alleviate that pain.

Think back to a time in your life when you were confronted with having to make a tough choice. If possible, pick one you agonized over. Do you recall how tiring it was standing at that crossroads? Being in limbo is exhausting! Now, think of how it felt when you finally made a choice, one way or the other. All of a sudden, the pressure was off and you were free of the anxiety that comes with the fear of making a mistake. But, in the meantime, you may have missed any number of opportunities to do other things while you were struggling to make a decision about that one thing. And, what of the person who doesn't choose, and instead waits for life to make the choice for her? While living by default may seem like a useful strategy, there's no power in it – no opportunity for growth and no possibility of change. The truth is that if you want to live powerfully, you have to choose consciously and on purpose. The truth is that life happens, regardless. As much as you may want to avoid making choices sometimes, eventually something WILL happen. You can either choose purposefully or be a victim of circumstance. And, remember that avoiding making a choice IS a choice. You can choose consciously or unconsciously, but you can never "not choose".

When I was in the process of choosing whether or not to stay in my marriage, choosing consciously was an especially sensitive issue for me. I knew that I wasn't happy in the marriage and I spiritually knew that leaving was the appropriate choice. Emotionally, however, I was not ready to make that choice, for several reasons. I was afraid a separation would render me financially unstable. I kept thinking that the relationship might be salvageable. I even entertained the thought that God would be upset with me if I left the person to whom I had promised "until death do us part". These thoughts bounced around in my head almost daily for several years before I finally decided to make a change. I'm sharing this here, not only to provide a real life example of choice versus no choice, but also to say that by taking no action, I effectively delayed my own spiritual and emotional growth. Although I understood that I was making choices that were not right for me spiritually, I chose to allow my fears to stop me. And, here, as they say, is the rub. While the marriage was unhappy, the real source of pain for me was the knowledge that I was choosing to stay in it rather than leave it. And, that knowledge, even more than the marriage, itself, is what finally led me to choose more powerfully. Perhaps if I had not understood the relationship between choice and suffering, I could have feigned ignorance. But I knew that avoiding making choices causes pain and suffering. And, now you know it, also.

How many times have you suffered over making a choice, afraid to move in a definitive direction, and then looked back with regret? We've all been there, and as hard as it is to admit we've made a mistake, there is absolutely no shame in choosing *badly*. In fact, being ashamed of our choices can cause us to keep making the same choices over and over again, because shame has the effect of rendering us unconscious to anything except the shame, making it less likely that we will actually learn from our mistakes. The thing to remember is that every choice is an opportunity to experience something new in life, an opportunity for growth, and an opportunity for life to teach us something. The only wrong choices are the ones we make unconsciously.

So, learn to make conscious choices - the easy ones and the hard ones. And when you do, ask yourself why you made the choice you made. Remember, the more you know about yourself, the more power you will have in the world. The more conscious you are about the choices you make, the more you will appreciate how your choices have shaped your life and you will have a better understanding of the power you have to change it. It's not unusual for women to stay in relationships because they believe they have no choice, but it just isn't true. At the writing of this book, my husband and I are creating a new structure for our relationship. That would not have happened had I not made a conscious choice to expand my own spiritual and emotional boundaries.

Choosing consciously is energizing, freeing, and empowering. Choosing unconsciously (failing to choose) is disempowering and increases your chances of falling victim to circumstances that may appear to be beyond your control, but in reality are not. Choosing consciously is a healing practice because it puts you squarely at the helm of your life. Not only will you no longer be a victim of your circumstances or relationships, but you will also be applying your personal power to dictate your own glorious future.

Healing Worksheet – Choosing Consciously

As you go throughout your day, practice making conscious choices. Remember that life presents us with a series of choices each and every day, some of which don't occur as choices, but if we pay attention, we can clearly see them as they are. Begin to notice when suffering is present and determine what you are or are not choosing that is causing the suffering. Notice the reasoning behind the choices you make, and acknowledge the consequences that come as a result.

Healing Questions to Promote Choosing Consciously

What are the choices I make every day? [Some may be obvious, e.g. when to rise in the morning, what to wear, what to eat, etc. Some are not so obvious, e.g. whether to be happy or not, how to react in the face of adversity, and how to conduct yourself in your life and relationships.]

Of the choices I make, which are conscious and which are unconscious?

How do the choices I make affect my life?

What can I do to ensure that I choose more consciously?

How would my life benefit from making more conscious choices?

Who will I be being? What might I do differently? What might I have that I don't have already?

Which one of my power centers is most activated by this conversation? (Spiritual, emotional, sensual, intellectual, intuitive?)

The Healing Practice of Taking Imperfect Action

Every action you take will lead you closer to your goal and consequently, closer to your abundant life. Unfortunately, instead of taking action, many people allow their reasons and excuses to keep them from moving forward. The truth is that the word *excuse* is just another word for *fear*! And fear is the number one reason that people don't take action, don't keep their promises, and don't live powerful lives. I let fear hold me back from living an authentic life for many years, before I learned to act in spite of my fear. It's true that living authentically can be a somewhat risky proposition. But failing to do so is spiritual and emotional suicide.

The acronym for fear is F-False E-Expectation A-Appearing R-Real. What this refers to is the fact that the source of all fear is a belief that something unpleasant will happen if we take a particular action.

Fear is a learned reaction – a result of past experiences, the memories of which remain in our subconscious and dictate the choices we make and the actions we take in the present.

Fear is also a survival tool. In prehistoric times, man feared being eaten by saber toothed tigers. Now the tigers exist in our minds, waiting to pounce on us whenever we venture outside of our comfort zones. As we know, life inside our comfort zones requires very little from us in the way of action. Instead, it allows us to operate largely on automatic pilot, making new action unnecessary or too uncomfortable to bear.

Have you ever promised yourself that you were going to lose weight, get more sleep, quit your job, or end a relationship and then made some excuse as to why it wasn't the right time? Not keeping your promises to yourself is a sure sign that fear is present. Have you ever blamed the circumstances or the people in your life for why you can't do something or why you don't have the life you want? Blaming others for the condition of your life is a sure sign that fear is present. The irony is that until you stop making excuses and start keeping your promises, your life will never change and you will be stuck dealing with the same issues over and over again. The same fears will continue to plague you and the same limiting beliefs will keep you from accomplishing anything new in your life.

Now, let me say a few words about something almost every woman grapples with. It's called perfection. The need to be perfect is fed by feelings of inadequacy and an irrational fear that if we're not careful, people will see that we're not as good as they think we are – that we'll be found out. In my experience, men do not have the same relationship with perfection as do women. One reason that women pursue perfection is systemic suppression. Unfortunately, living in a male-dominant society has taught women over time that to be female is to be flawed. Women are consistently undervalued in the workplace, underrepresented in positions of power, and often underestimated in society as a whole. In many parts of the world, women who own and express their power are often met with resistance, stereotyped as the emasculating female, or labeled as "overly emotional". The United States is no exception.

It's no wonder that so many women feel it necessary to hide their true power or attempt to change who they are in order to fit into careers and relationships that demand they be both strong and weak, both aggressive and diminutive, sexy but not too sexy, smart but not too smart. A woman's life can be very confusing, especially in light of the fact that none of society's conflicting messages are in any way authentic to women themselves. Rather, they are messages that have been perpetrated by a male-dominant society to perpetuate the status quo – woman as caretaker, sex object, subservient and less valuable entity. A woman's need to appear perfect and have her "ducks in a row" before taking action is a syndrome that is, in large part, driven by this perpetration - internalized shame, stemming from male-dominant socialization; and stands squarely in the way of her spiritual, emotional, and even financial development. The remedy for this syndrome is the willingness to take what is called "imperfect action".

Imperfect action is action that is either not completely thought out, or thought out enough to be clear but not enough to have all the bells and whistles attached to it. It's not the same as impulsive action, which can be, and usually is, unconscious in nature. Imperfect action is not only conscious – it's purposeful. The Nike slogan, "Just Do It" comes to mind. Just take action. This is especially important for women who are interested in building a business or increasing their visibility in the world. Putting oneself "out there" is always going to feel risky and fear of failure or fear of being ridiculed for one's ideas is common. I've certainly felt that way many times in my own career. But, I know that my ability to make an impact in the world requires me to share my knowledge and my talents, and there's no guarantee that everyone I share with will agree with what I have to say. In fact, it's pretty well guaranteed that they will not. Some time ago one of my coaches taught me a very valuable lesson. What she said was that often people want to "hear the angels singing" before they take action. People don't understand that the angels only sing after we take action, and not before. That lesson was life-changing for me, because I realized that I had been delaying putting many of my ideas into action, waiting for the perfect moment, the perfect opportunity, the perfect me. I clearly understood that by not being in action, I was sabotaging my results, but I lacked the tools to move beyond those thoughts. I was waiting to be perfect! If you've been putting off action in favor of perfection, stop it! You're wasting valuable time!

Perfection is a myth that will always leave you wanting. No matter how good a job you do, there will always be something else you could have done. The truth is that the best you can do is the best you can do, and the best you can do is enough. If you're someone who lacks confidence, taking imperfect action can enhance your faith in your abilities. While fear creates inertia and an experience of being stuck, action creates momentum and an experience of accomplishment. The more action you take, the less fearful you'll become, as you realize that what you feared would happen is not even a remote possibility. In other words, the closer you step towards it, the less real fear becomes and the more powerful you become. Consequently, the more accomplished you feel, the more energy you will have for taking repetitive action. Unfortunately, human beings are so conditioned to avoid discomfort (for good reason) that one could live a lifetime without ever taking a risk. That is why it's important for you to be able to monitor your internal conversations and interrupt them before they paralyze you. It isn't that you will ever be fearless. Fear is always there, lurking in the background. It's just the nature of being human. Understanding the difference between fear and fact, and acting in spite of your fear is the only way to loosen its grip on your emotions and your behaviors.

The easiest way to tell that you are having a fear-based conversation is hearing the little voice in your head telling you that you aren't good enough, or smart enough, or whatever enough to take a particular action. I call that the voice of your saboteur. You could also call that the voice of your ego or your past. Either way, its design is to make sure you don't do anything that would make you uncomfortable in any way. To your ego, discomfort is dangerous, and it will lie to you to keep you safe. It's not true that you are not good enough. There is no certainty that something bad will happen if you make a particular choice or take a particular action; but if you are not practiced at facing down your ego it will not only run the show; it will run away with your life. "Edging Out God" is an acronym that is used by some when discussing the characteristics of the ego. Your ego's only purpose is to keep you alive. It has no interest in your growth and development and is not aligned with your divine essence.

That is why it is so important to begin to recognize when your ego (saboteur) begins to whisper all those lies in your ear that make you believe you don't have what it takes to get what you want. While it may be protecting you from unknown consequences, your ego stands squarely in the way of your spiritual development. In order to be powerful, you must learn to "sideline" your "saboteur".

So, how do you do that? The first thing to do is to recognize fear-based conversation. Fear-based conversations often occur in our blind spots, so unless you are willing to make the effort to observe your thoughts and behavior patterns you may never realize that fear is running the show. It may surprise you to know that excuses such as, "not enough time" and "not enough money" are fear- based conversations. In fact, time and money are the two most common fear-based excuses people give for not being in action, and you should be on the lookout for them in your own life. The next time you find yourself using these or any other excuse for not doing something you know you want to do, check in with yourself to see if the reason you're making the excuse is because you are afraid to take the intended action. Really, check it out! Fear of failure, fear of rejection, and fear of the un- known are some common themes behind the excuses people give for not following through.

The other thing to do is to have faith. If you have an idea, go with it. If you have a desire, go after it. If you have a dream, go for it! Act in faith that all things work for the good, and that anything you put out into the world with the intention of moving it (or you) in a positive direction will meet with positive energy in the universe and be carried forward. The lessons to be learned from taking imperfect action are many and the benefits are huge! There is a saying, "leap and the net will appear". Imperfect action teaches us that the universe will support us if we only dare to step out of our own way and it rewards us handsomely when we do. The only thing you have to lose is time, and time is a precious thing, indeed.

The next time you find yourself making excuses for why you aren't living powerfully, instead of backing off, take your fear by the hand and get into action. The more action you take, the less fear you will feel and the less resistance you will experience. Susan Jeffers has written a landmark book on the subject of fear, which I highly recommend. It's called, *Feel the Fear and Do It Anyway,* and its inspirational message is powerfully transformative.

Taking imperfect action and acting in spite of fear are healing practices because they make it possible to move forward in life in spite of one's circumstances, beliefs, and perceptions. Fear is pervasive and it can potentially hold you hostage unless you recognize it for what it is and take the action necessary to live the powerful life you want and deserve. There is no such thing as perfection, and to pursue it is a waste of time and energy. Instead of spending spiritual and emotional energy on "getting your ducks in a row", do yourself a favor. Leap! I promise, the net will appear.

Healing Worksheet –
Taking Imperfect Action

Begin to notice which reasons and excuses you use most often for not taking action and determine what you are trying to avoid by your inaction. Be honest with yourself. It's alright to be afraid. It's healing to act in spite of your fear. Remember, any action is better than no action!

Healing Questions to Promote Imperfect Action

Where am I not taking action in my life? Where have I broken my promises to myself? Where am I trying to be perfect and why?

What am I afraid will happen if I take imperfect action in my life?

What imperfect actions can I take that will make a difference in my life and/or in the world?

How will taking imperfect action benefit my life?

Who will I be being? What might I do differently? What might I have that I don't have already?

Which one of my power centers is most activated by this conversation? (Spiritual, emotional, sensual, intellectual, intuitive?)

The Healing Practice of Full Self-Expression

The healing practice of being self-expressed is arguably the most important of all, because only by expressing yourself fully will you experience all of who you are. Each aspect of your personality is a gift. Each one of them is unique and each one of them is divinely purposed. That is why you will never achieve your full purpose if you are not willing to know who you are and love who you are enough to be yourself, express yourself and speak your truth in the world. I know that sounds harsh, but I want to be sure that you understand the gravity involved here.

You are more than your job, more than your relationships, and more than your daily routine might suggest. And, it's only by exploring the true nature of your being – your likes and dislikes, what you want and what you are good at – that you will discover who you really are and what you are here for. Self-expression is considered to be a right in this country. But, not all women are encouraged or even allowed to speak their minds or pursue their dreams; in many societies, authentic self-expression is just not an option. The suppression of female voices is not just a tragedy for women, but for their families, communities, and society, as a whole. I suggest, therefore, that speaking up, daring to follow your heart, and spending time doing what makes you happy are not so much rights as they are privileges, and in many ways, an obligation.

Those of us for whom full self-expression is an option must be role models. Our daughters depend on us to demonstrate the behaviors we want them to emulate, and too often what we say to them is not always matched by what we do for them and for ourselves. By nature, women are healers and nurturers, and we have a responsibility to share our knowledge and our strength with others, which only happens when we share our gifts. No matter what your cultural, professional, or educational background or orientation, when you honor your own voice and allow yourself to explore the edges of your self-expression, in whatever form that takes, you become a leader – not only in your life, but in the world.

Each of us blocks our self-expression from time to time for any number of reasons, and the tendency is to think that tomorrow will be soon enough to do what we want, say what we want, and have what we want.

Unfortunately for many people, tomorrow never comes and opportunities are wasted. You'll never have what you want if you don't pursue it, and you'll never know what you're capable of unless you act boldly and dream big. Self-expression is the key to manifestation. That which you speak and act on with devotion will manifest in the world and give you your reality. Every time you speak your truth in the world you align your intentions with the universe and generate positive energy around your vision and your divine purpose. When you express yourself, you not only allow others to know you and benefit from your knowledge, you also receive a deeper understanding and appreciation for who you are and what you have to offer. Writing, creating art of any kind, working and teaching are all avenues of both self- expression and self-discovery – leading you to new insights and new ways of thinking and behaving. As you expand your capabilities, you also call new opportunities for expansion into your life.

Sometimes people are afraid to learn about themselves, even when they intuitively know that the life they are living is not authentic for them. Self-discovery can feel like risky business, especially when you've conditioned the people in your life to interact with you as the person you've been being, and when expressing yourself authentically may threaten the status quo.

Some time ago, I designed and led a course titled, *Write for Power: Uncover, Heal, and Step into Your*

Victorious Life. In that course, I introduced women to the power of sharing their stories and took them through the stages of writing a transformational book based on their experiences. For some of them, this was a frightening proposition. Writing about life experiences conjures up latent memories and emotions that are unpleasant, to say the least, and some of the women expressed worry that once they opened the door to those suppressed emotions, they would not be able to close it. But, through the process of writing about their experiences, they were able to see how the trials they had lived through, although painful, had contributed to who they were as women, and sourced their commitments, values, and strengths. Through the sharing of their stories, the women in my program were able to transform limiting beliefs, connect with their most authentic voice and express that voice in the world. The result was the successful transformation of their pain into powerful inspiration for making a difference in the world and for helping other women who had lived through similar circumstances. While not all of the women who took the course became or will become best-selling authors, by transforming their experience of the past, each woman gained a powerful perspective from which to create a future that is based on who she is and what she wants, rather than on her limiting beliefs about what is possible. This is the power of writing. It helps you discover who you really are.

This was certainly my experience. With each of my books, I discovered a different aspect of myself. By sharing my personal experiences for the benefit of other women, I transformed them from sources of pain to sources of power. Writing to make an impact has helped me to find a path and a purpose that wasn't available to me before, and that I now feel confident in traveling. Without the writing, that would not have happened.

I had been thinking about writing a book for years before I actually completed one. I suspect there are some of you who have also been thinking about writing a book, and that's good. The difference between thinking and writing is that there is a transformative quality to the act of writing. Whether you write by hand or on a keyboard, there is something about seeing the words and feeling them flow out of you and onto the page that brings about spiritual expansion. Writing puts you more in touch with your feelings, which is why many people don't actually write, although they think about it frequently. It's the divine connection within us that knows writing will somehow free us up to live a more empowered life, but it's our own limited thinking – that saboteur – that keeps us from taking the leap. People don't like to feel the rush of emotions that often comes with recalling painful events. It's uncomfortable and makes us feel vulnerable. What's true, however, is that until we are able to revisit and reframe those events, they will continue to serve as roadblocks to healing and personal empowerment. Should you take on this type of project, it will be important for you to maintain your emotional boundaries as much as possible – writing and remembering only as far as you feel comfortable at any given time. You can always pick up where you left off the next time you sit down to write. Pushing yourself, while therapeutic in some respects, can be dangerous. Only write what you are ready to write, but write. Consider it a gift to yourself.

No one has to see what you write. Your stories are yours and yours alone, and I recommend that you only share them with people you trust to keep them sacred. I promise you that even if you never share a single story, that recalling the experiences of your life and writing them down will help you connect with your authentic self, identify your personal truth, and find your most authentic voice. One of the lessons I share with my classes is that whatever you don't resolve in adolescence and young adulthood will come back to haunt you in your 40's and 50's. This phenomenon is a natural part of a woman's life. As we enter middle age we are somehow able to hear the universe calling to us more clearly. The voice of our higher self grows louder as we are called to serve the purpose for which we were born. It's during this time that we are reminded of old wounds, unresolved issues, and unlived dreams. For women, middle age is a time in our lives where we begin to assess the fruits of our labor and wonder what we will do with the next 50 years. If we are wise, we will look back on our lives with admiration for ourselves, our accomplishments, and the people we've encountered over the years. But, whether we look back in celebration or sorrow, middle age for women is a time of self-reflection and re-direction. Most of all, it is a time where faith is of great importance and our relationship to divine guidance is stronger than at any other time in life.

It's not unusual for women in this stage of life to find fault with their current realities – to struggle with careers and relationships that no longer serve them. Like seedlings struggling to break through the earth, women in their late 40's and 50's are called to break free of the limitations of social and emotional bonds that have defined them and seek opportunities for spiritual growth and expansion. Some leave their spouses, start new businesses, and take on new spiritual practices. For women, middle age is a time of rebirth. It's a time when we stop caring what other people think and devote our lives to doing the things that are closest to our hearts.

A favorite poem of mine is by an anonymous author who writes about the irrepressible rage of a menopausal woman and the voice that will not be denied.

We're all in this together, that's for sure. It's our duty to support each other, to help each other find our most authentic voices and live the purpose for which we were born. It's our job to educate, motivate, and inspire each other toward greatness and to appreciate each other's journeys.

But, writing is not exclusionary; writing is transformative, regardless of what you write about. You can connect more deeply with yourself by writing about current events, as well as past experiences. By recording your thoughts and your feelings in the present, you come face to face with who you are being in every moment, and that is of extreme value! So write on! There is nothing to fear! Whether you journal or blog, write a memoir, a short story, or a poem, there is healing and power in every word you write! You will gain courage, strength, clarity, and a sense of purpose. As you connect more deeply with your truth, you will find yourself able to walk in it and speak it into the world. At any and all of these moments, you not only invite transformation into your life, you bring it to others.

Of course, writing is only one form of self-expression. Participation in any of the artistic outlets can be equally as transformative when done on a regular basis. It is a well-known fact among transformational experts that lasting change cannot be obtained through thought alone. There must be corresponding behaviors that accompany thought in order for new neural pathways to be formed. New ways of thinking are granted us only when we adopt new ways of behaving. We covered this in the chapter that addressed the healing power of taking imperfect action. This assumption is evidenced by the effectiveness of therapeutic modalities that use dance, art, and music to help people heal from trauma of all types. Painting, singing, and dancing are all examples of activities that you might use to access your truth and expand your capacity for self-expression.

Other suggestions are taking up a new sport, hiking, biking or walking in nature. One thing to note here is that nature and art of any kind, in and of themselves, are transformative; even just going out into nature, surrounding yourself with art, listening to soothing music, or reading transformational materials will help you connect more deeply with your spirit and with your authentic voice. Of course, meditation, yoga, and other alternative healing practices are always recommended, and are usually very effective at helping people break through to higher levels of thought and spiritual healing. And, if you're really ready to let yourself be seen, become a speaker, teach a course, or lead a workshop of your own. I promise, there will always be someone who wants and needs to hear what you have to say.

Being self-expressed is a healing practice because it is one of the keys to self-expansion and fulfillment. It's how you will accomplish your biggest achievements. It's also how you will make your biggest impact in the world. There is no joy in living under the radar. Speak out, live big, and be happy. The world is drawn to people who aren't afraid to express themselves. It's enlightening and empowering to be around that kind of energy. You can create that energy for yourself, if you're willing to be your authentic self and allow yourself to enjoy all the benefits that come along with that!

Healing Worksheet – Self-Expression

Speak your truth. Say what is real for you. Ask for what you need. Spend time nurturing yourself. Do something that brings joy to your life. Share your gifts. Follow your dreams. Look for opportunities to contribute your ideas. Be creative. Step out of the shadows and into the limelight. Play a bigger game!

Healing Questions to Promote Self-Expression

Where in my life am I not expressing myself fully or speaking my truth?

Where in my life am I not asking for what I want and/or need?

What gifts do I have that I am not sharing?

Where in my life am I playing small / flying under the radar?

What might be a bigger game for me to play and how would my life be affected by my playing it?

What actions can I take to nurture myself and bring joy into my life?

What actions can I take to deepen my spiritual connection and find my most authentic voice?

How will my life be affected by my having a deeper connection to my most authentic self?

Who will I be being? What might I do differently? What might I have that I don't have already?

Which one of my power centers is most activated by this conversation? (Spiritual, emotional, sensual, intellectual, intuitive?)

The Healing Practice
of Letting Go

I've never been good at letting go, but I know I'm not alone. People like to hold on to things. Memories, feelings, relationships and circumstances are a few examples of things people like to hang on to, sometimes longer than is good for us. Jim Rohn said "You're the average of the five people you spend the most time with". For some of us, that's the bad news; for others, it's not so bad. Either way, it's a good idea to take inventory once in a while just to be sure that the people you're surrounding yourself with are a positive influence on your life. It's a bad idea to stay in relationships with people who either bring negativity into your life or mirror your own negativity in ways that keep you stuck. The same rule applies to circumstances, emotions, and memories that we may perpetuate, but that drag us down, rather than lift us up.

Something most people don't know, that it's important for you to understand, is that the Universe sends us people to teach us what we need to learn in order to move forward in life. We are not always meant to stay in relationship with those people our entire lives. Some people are just meant to stay with us for a season and move on. Often the people we learn the most from are people who have similar issues to our own; they act as mirrors for us to see who we are being and what we are doing to hold ourselves back. If you notice that the people in your life appear to have the same or similar issues, pay attention. Those people are there to teach you something you need to know about yourself or about life, and you won't stop meeting those types of people until you learn your lesson and move on.

The same is true of your circumstances; we're meant to learn from our situations and grow to the next level, not hang out in them endlessly. Again, it's about self-awareness. Notice who and what is around you. Use your intuition to recognize how your relationships and circumstances are affecting you and vice versa. Often we resist learning the lessons being offered and stay in relationships long after they've served their purpose. Learning to recognize when to let go is critical to being able to progress along your spiritual path. If your circumstances are less than great, ask yourself what you're there to learn so you can get to what's next in your life. If your relationships don't inspire you to be your best self, it may be time to let some of them go.

Yes, it's hard to let go of people who've become important to you, but you owe it to yourself to assess whether or not those people are a healthy influence. Don't let the people in your life make you crazy! It's just not worth it, especially if those relationships are causing you pain!

Hanging out in hurtful relationships suggests codependency. So, how do you know if you're in a codependent relationship? Well, there are degrees of codependency. Not all codependent relationships are unhappy, but most of them are less than fulfilling. Many codependent people have low self-esteem, feel they are inadequate, and have trouble liking themselves. Many are perfectionists, concerned with how others view them. Codependent people often lack assertiveness, have difficulty expressing their own needs, and have trouble saying "no". The chances are that you know at least one person who fits this description. You don't have to know them well to recognize these sorts of behaviors.

Once again, we're talking about boundaries. If you find yourself taking on other people's problems, being drawn into other people's upsets, or unable to draw the line between your own needs and someone else's, you're in codependency territory. The same is true if you're in relationship with someone who has the characteristics I described. If this is the case, consider that the relationship isn't serving either one of you. Codependent people look to others to facilitate their healing, and that's just not how it works. Again, watch yourself in action. If you think you may be codependent, you owe it to yourself to learn more about it. Most people are a bit codependent. It's human nature. It only becomes a problem when it's the basis for relationship, rather than an aspect of it. Again, codependency occurs in degrees. It helps to be mindful of the fact that people derive value from codependency; codependent relationships reinforce old stories, and allow people to perpetuate personal dysfunction.

The relationship with the man I lived with after college was incredibly codependent. He had low self-esteem and so did I, but not knowing anything about codependency at the time, I just thought that if I worked hard enough and loved him enough, that we would be happy together. I could never have anticipated that three years later we would still be struggling. Well, I was struggling. He was living the good life, because I was taking care of him. Usually, in codependent relationships, one person gives and the other takes. In my relationships, I was almost always the giver, and this one was no exception. The other thing about codependent relationships is that the giver tends to give to the point of sacrifice and the taker has no problem with that arrangement. Again, this isn't always true, but it often is. This particular man couldn't keep a job, so I paid all the bills. He didn't have a reliable car, so I let him use mine. I knew I was unhappy, but I kept thinking we could work it out. The value that I had been generating for myself (and what kept me in the relationship) was the sense of being needed. As long as I was taking care of him I felt like I had a purpose. At the time, I wasn't familiar with the concept of enabling. How helpful it would have been if I had been able to see him for who he was, and to see who I was being in the relationship. Perhaps if I had understood that my own lack of self-esteem was driving me to support him rather than myself, I wouldn't have wasted so much time. Truth be told, it was actually he rather than I who finally walked away.

After we parted, I spent quite some time working through the details of the relationship, trying to understand what had happened and why I had been so willing to forfeit my happiness. What I now understand is that he had a very poor relationship with himself as a person, and all the love in the world was not going to change that for him. What I learned from my relationship with him was that I would have to manage my relationship with myself in order to find happiness. Until that time, I had not realized how low my sense of self-worth really was and I had to learn to rectify that if I was ever going to escape the lure of codependency. Not only did I have to let go of the relationship, I had to let go of my need to be loved and learn to love myself instead.

One of the most important things to know about letting go is that it frees us up to see what's stopping us in life. Holding onto that dysfunctional relationship allowed me to blame someone else for my unhappiness. Letting go allowed me to see that it was me all along, standing in my own way, keeping me from stepping out and using my power to cause my own happiness instead of someone else's. If you think you are in a codependent relationship, it's ultimately up to you to do the work to see what's keeping you stuck and then do whatever you have to do to break out of that dysfunction. Once free, it's your obligation to acknowledge the lessons learned, and apply them to your life in a way that helps you see yourself in action, so you can make better choices.

Again, my situation was fairly extreme, but there's a point to be made in my sharing it. Co-dependencies occur in all sorts of situations. It's possible to have codependent relationships with coworkers, parents, children, and best friends. It's not so much a matter of the type of relationships, as it is a matter of how people relate to each other inside of them. If a relationship isn't working, for whatever reason, you owe it to yourself to take a step back from it and look at it as objectively as you can. Ask yourself if you are getting what you need in the relationship. Are you happy? Is your partner happy? Often people stay in relationships because they don't want to be alone, or they feel that they've invested too much time and they don't want to start over. Perhaps you see that your relationship with one or more of your family members is codependent. I've been there, and I know it's hard to walk away from people we care about and perhaps have built a life with. And, you don't have to. Transformation is possible, but it requires honesty. If you're in one or more relationships that aren't exactly working for you, check your boundaries. Are you getting as much as you are giving and vice versa? Are you waiting for other people to make you happy? Do you notice yourself becoming frustrated, upset, or angry when you are together? If so, you might consider that the lesson you were meant to learn from this person is complete, and it might be time to move on. In the case of family members, it may be time to separate yourself from them emotionally – in order to keep from being drawn into drama, for example, or to declare your independence so you can be less reliant on them. Whatever you choose, you'll be choosing consciously. Whether you let go of the relationship or not, you'll be looking with fresh eyes, and that's powerful!

Letting go is a healing practice, because it opens our eyes to where we've been stuck and frees us up to move forward in life. Often people operate inside of an illusion when it comes to their relationships. They don't have a clear picture of who they're being and how their actions are contributing to dysfunction. People who let go of situations and relationships that don't serve them enjoy a greater sense of freedom and self-worth, which they express in their relationships and pass on to others. They see the value in the lesson and move on when the lesson is complete. Letting go is a practice that ultimately allows us to experience more of who we are spiritually. It helps us move through emotional baggage, and opens us up to receive love and to experience peace of mind and an abundant life.

Healing Worksheet – Letting Go

Take inventory of your relationships and assess whether or not they support your needs and the needs of those with whom you are in relationship. Begin to notice yourself in action in your relationships. Are they causing you upset? Are you settling for less than you want? Are you in touch with your emotions? Are you fully self-expressed? Are you overly accommodating? These are just some of the questions you can ask that will help you determine whether or not it is time to separate yourself emotionally from someone (or something) or let go completely.

Healing Questions to Facilitate Letting Go

Am I happy in my relationships / Am I waiting or others to make me happy?

Do I feel fully respected, loved, and appreciated?

Are my relationships serving me and the people with whom I am in relationship?

Do I feel like it's OK for me to say no in my relationships?

Have I been hanging out in bad situations that no longer serve my purpose? If so, which ones?

Do I allow others to dictate my actions / Do I feel comfortable being autonomous in my relationships?

Which relationships / situations might I want to look at to assess codependency?

How might I benefit from learning to let go?

Who will I be being? What might I do differently? What might I have that I don't have already?

Which one of my power centers is most activated by this conversation? (Spiritual, emotional, sensual, intellectual, intuitive?)

The Healing Practice
of Self-Care

Before I became a life coach, I was working as a certified personal fitness trainer. My specialty was helping women between the ages of 35 and 65 reclaim their bodies from injury, illness, and neglect. When I first started training, I believed what I had been taught. Health and fitness is all about what you eat and how much you exercise, right? Well, yes and no. Managing caloric intake and expenditure is certainly one component of a healthy lifestyle, but it's not the entire picture. Health and fitness also has a huge emotional and spiritual component. For women and men alike, it's not just about what we eat and how much we exercise. Optimal health and well-being is also about how we feel about ourselves. It's about whether or not we enjoy our careers and our relationships and how we view the world. What that means is that both wellness and disease have emotional components to them. When women don't take care of themselves emotionally, their bodies suffer. When they don't take care of their bodies, their spirits suffer. It's no secret that illnesses such as diabetes, arthritis, obesity, fibromyalgia, and various digestive disorders, as well as anxiety, insomnia, and depression can be helped or cured through sustained self-care. For many women, this means facing down fears, getting over feelings of unworthiness, and breaking through the limiting beliefs that have taken hold after years of self-neglect. I know this because in all the years I worked as a trainer, I never had a client who didn't come face to face with her emotional baggage on the road to physical health. One of the reasons for this is because most, if not all, women have a love-hate relationship with their bodies. We have stories about how our bodies should look and how they should function; many women are ashamed of their bodies, not because they are unattractive, but because society has taught us that we should be ashamed. Remember Adam and the fig leaf? The bottom line is that optimal health depends on physical, emotional, and spiritual well-being and can only be obtained by addressing all three. One of the most valuable lessons I learned as a trainer is that when women listen to their bodies, they can heal their hearts, and when they listen to their hearts, they can heal their bodies.

In this chapter on self-care, I'll touch back on some of the things I discussed in previous chapters, so there may be some repetition. But, trust me, this is not a chapter you want to skip. How you feel about and care for your body is going to be a huge factor in your ability to heal, grow, and thrive. If you're not taking care of yourself physically or ignoring your spiritual, emotional, or intellectual needs, you may be hampering your ability to heal.

Not only is your body the vessel that houses your spirit, but the body and the spirit have a symbiotic relationship. Healthy bodies support healthy spirits and vice versa. If you're not currently checking in with your body and giving it what it's asking for, I recommend you start as soon as possible. If you don't currently have a self- care program, you'll want to be sure that you create one, and this chapter can help you to do that.

Imagine that you are a gardener, sowing the seeds for your spiritual expansion. In order for the seeds to take root, you first need to prepare the soil with fertilizer. Then you need to provide plenty of water and warmth. Once the seeds sprout and the shoots break the soil, you continue to nurture them with water and sunlight and protect them from the elements. In this scenario, you are encouraging your spiritual flowers to grow. You would certainly not dig the seeds up before they sprout, or step on the new shoots, or even trim the heads off the buds before they bloom. But this is what many people do, where their spiritual growth is concerned.

One of the joys of my life is teaching yoga to middle-aged women who are re-inventing themselves in some way. Whether shifting careers, changing relationships, or adjusting to their bodies' hormonal fluctuations, what is common for these women is that at some time or another they have become disconnected from their spiritual center and they're ready to come back home. They have paid their dues in terms of supporting the people they care about, and they are ready to step into their spiritual purpose. In each session I encourage them to quiet their minds and go into their bodies in order to connect more deeply with their divine source, to rediscover their passion, and to call on the wisdom of their intuition. In this way, I help them discover their truth. Often in this process, memories come to the surface, and emotions come flooding in. Their natural reaction is to try to push them back down through denial or rationalization. During these times, I invite them to notice what's happening inside their bodies, to acknowledge the feeling of fight or flight, and to breathe through it rather than react to it.

Being present to the physical body is an integral part of the healing process. Remember that your physical body is the vessel for your spiritual body. In order for your spirit to expand and grow, you must be able to fully occupy your body, and the most effective way to do that is to breathe – slowly, deeply, and consciously. The process of connecting with your body, getting present to what's happening for you in the moment, acknowledging your emotions, and embracing the sum total of your life experiences are key to living a powerful life. This is the gift of mindfulness, being present in the moment, and noticing the world around you while holding the space for your own growth and healing.

We all have emotional triggers – thoughts and experiences that set us off on life's emotional rollercoaster. It's natural to want to protect yourself, but when you judge and suppress your feelings you also deny yourself the right and the opportunity to be whoever and however you are being at the time. Remember, although we are earthly beings, the nature of our life purpose is spiritual, and spiritual suppression has consequences. Unless you allow your spirit to be fully expressed, your purpose cannot be revealed and you will miss much of what is available to you in life.

It's nonetheless useful to know what your emotional triggers are so you aren't blindsided by your own emotions. The next time you find yourself in an emotional breakdown, ask yourself what set it off and make a mental note. Seeing the source of our upsets is all part of the enlightenment process. Allowing yourself to experience the upset with no loss of enthusiasm is empowering and it represents a step forward in the healing process.

Another critically important piece of your self-care program will be to stop being all things to all people. In other words, Just Say No! It's no secret that women tend to take on way too much. And, many of the things we take on are in the interest of taking care of the people we care about, which may leave little time for doing the things that contribute to our well-being, as well as everybody else's. If you've been burning the candle at both ends, spending a lot of time putting out fires, or generally pretending to be Superwoman, it might be time for you to take off the "S". It's just not appropriate for you to take on the world unless you can take care of yourself at the same time. Practicing self-care is a critical component of healing and an important part of the empowerment process. If you're serious about healing your power, you're going to have to take time for yourself and start to delegate some of those tasks on your to-do list to someone else, or take them off the list altogether. If you're a single parent, working two jobs, or going back to school, etc. this might sound like an impossible task. But taking 5 minutes to sit quietly and do nothing can go a long way toward rejuvenation and it's a perfectly valid first step to taking back your power. Saying "no" takes practice, so be patient, but also be resolute. After all, "NO!" is a complete sentence! It requires no explanation or embellishment. Yes, it takes courage and a good deal of commitment to make yourself a priority in your own life, but it's worth it. I promise!

Your mission, should you decide to accept it, is to either begin a self-care program or enhance the one you have. The first thing to do is to check in with your body and inquire as to what it needs. Make a list of the items that you feel need to be addressed. What does your body need in order to feel good, look good, and serve its (your) higher purpose? To help you get started, I've listed some suggestions, but you may want to enlist the help of a trainer, yoga instructor, nutritionist, physician, or alternative health practitioner. There is no shame in asking for support, in fact, it's the right thing to do if you're starting something new, especially if you've been procrastinating about doing so. It's incredible how attached women seem to be to doing things all on our own, as if asking for help suggests weakness. The truth is that we are all works in progress and it's wise to understand that there is strength in numbers. While my personal training clients might have gotten the results they were looking for without my help, it would have taken them a whole lot longer, and it would not have been nearly as much fun!

Self-care is a healing practice because it helps bring into focus the sacred nature of the human body. By honoring your physical and emotional needs, you set your spirit free, as well. Whether you're dealing with serious health issues or not, it's imperative that you listen to your body and care for it with love. It's the only one you have. It's the only vessel your spirit will ever have, at least during this lifetime.

Healing Worksheet – Self-Care

Here is a list of general self-care categories for you to consider including in your personal self-care program. I've included some useful information, but my recommendation is that you seek support in the form of a personal trainer, registered dietician, or wellness coach. My experience is that when we seek support in any new endeavor we not only achieve our desired results, we stick to the program and continue to reap the benefits long into the future. However, the information I'm sharing here is basic enough that you can get started right away and continue on your own and still achieve good results.

Sleep – The human body needs 7-8 hours of sleep for every 24-hour cycle. If you're an early riser, that means going to bed earlier. Regardless of whether you're working or playing, burning the midnight oil is not good for your body. Neither is working online immediately before going to bed; electronic energy inhibits relaxation. The practice I recommend to my clients is to shut down all electronic devices by 10 pm and be in bed by 11. You'll find that giving your body enough rest affords you more energy to do the things you love and a greater capacity for doing the things you don't. Being well-rested also helps to regulate your metabolism.

When you sleep the recommended number of hours per night you'll burn more fat, your tissues will hold less fluid, and you'll be less likely to binge eat. Not only that, your mind will be clearer and you'll feel more alive and much less stressed.

Hydration –A healthy fluid intake for human beings includes a minimum of 32–64 ounces of water per day. When I say this to clients, they often look at me like I'm crazy. They literally think their kidneys will explode if they drink that much water. The fact is that a healthy metabolism depends on adequate hydration. When hydration levels are inadequate, your metabolism slows down, your mind and body get sluggish, and you feel tired and worn down. This is in part due to the buildup of toxins in the blood. When you drink the prescribed amounts of water, your liver is better able to do its job of filtering the blood, your digestive functions improve, and systemic inflammation is reduced. If you do nothing else to ensure proper nutrition, drinking at least 32 ounces of water will help increase your overall well-being on all levels. That's only four 8 oz. glasses. I'm pretty sure you can handle that. You just need to be intentional. Remember the chapter about self- awareness?

Nutrition – Recommendations for achieving a nutritional balance include eliminating white flour, white sugar and wheat products from your diet, reducing your intake of processed (packaged) foods and dairy products, opting for leaner protein sources, consuming a diet the majority of which is made up of green vegetables, and eating organic whenever possible. If this sounds like too much to take on, you don't have to do it all at one time. Taking on even one of these healthy practices will go a long way toward improving, not only your physical well-being, but your spiritual, intellectual, emotional, and intuitive well-being, as well. The best option for optimizing your nutrition is to hire a nutritionist or registered dietitian. However, there may be some local resources you can take advantage of; hospitals, health food stores, and doctors' offices often host wellness events and/or ongoing classes. There are also some very helpful resources online.

Exercise – The minimum recommendation for a healthy exercise routine is 30–60 minutes every other day. A better recommendation is 30–60 minutes daily. The good news is that it can be almost any kind of exercise, as long as it increases oxygen intake by elevating your respiration and heart rate. It almost doesn't matter what type of exercise you choose. They all have their merits, and you might want to experiment with several until you find the one that's best for you.

Of course, it's always advisable for you to check with your doctor before doing any strenuous exercise, especially if you haven't been exercising. Again, keep in mind that hiring a trainer or joining some organized fitness classes can help you stay accountable. You might also consider teaming up with a friend. It's more fun and you can support each other, while you're at it. There are also plenty of free fitness plans and exercise videos online, so there's really no excuse. Once again, a healthy body is the home of a healthy spirit. When you take care of your body you will experience heightened levels of energy, vitality, clarity, optimism, sensuality, and focus.

Mindfulness – Being intentionally aware of what you are doing in the present, rather than letting your mind wander from the task at hand. Often, people go through life on automatic pilot, moving from one task to another without thought or attention. When they place their attention on what they are doing, however, that act (no matter how simple or complicated) becomes one of transformation. It's well-known that the practices of yoga, qi gong, meditation and others like them quiet the mind and shift the autonomic nervous system away from fight or flight and towards rest and rejuvenation.

These same benefits are available in the simple act of attending to each task as if it were the most important task of the moment (which it is) and keeping your attention in the present. In this age of multi-tasking, being mindful is more than a notion.

An excellent place to begin a mindfulness practice is while you are eating. Mindless eating, binging, or eating too quickly causes overeating, stress, obesity, gastrointestinal upset and diabetes, among other ailments. By eating more slowly, placing your attention on what you are eating – how it looks, what it tastes like, the sensations of chewing and swallowing – you can actually enhance your digestive functioning, reduce cravings, and maintain a stable body weight. As you are ready, you can extend your mindfulness practice to other daily activities, like walking, bathing, and brushing your teeth. Notice the sensation of your feet hitting the ground, the water on your skin, the toothbrush as it touches your tongue. If you're inspired by the possibility of living in the moment, these simple acts can increase your capacity to do so, exponentially.

I hope you'll try this and all of the other self-care practices contained in this chapter, and that you'll be inspired to honor and care for your body. I also encourage you to share what you've learned with the other women in your circle. Remember, we are all in this together.

Closing Words

Heal Your Power, Heal Your Life presents you with a formula for self-empowerment and an invitation for you to step into your greatness. When you understand that your power in the present is contingent on your willingness to drop the constraints of past experiences and break through the barriers of self-imposed limitation, you will dream bigger and reach higher. You will also increase your ability to access your most authentic self, to discover your true purpose, and to express your gifts in the world.

Whether you know it or not, you have greatness within you, and you now have a formula for accessing that greatness. My hope is that you will adopt these new practices into your life and that you will use them to empower yourself to live authentically, passionately, fully expressed and fully actualized in your purpose.

I would also remind you not to lose sight of who you are and what you want out of life. Healing happens when you intentionally seek it, empower yourself to receive it, and allow your actions to be informed by its presence in your life. By intentionally seeking out healing practices and integrating those practices into your life, you bring power to your life and light to the world.

Thank you for being someone who is willing to Heal Your Power and Heal Your Life! I honor you and am grateful to have had the opportunity to support you on your journey to healing and self-empowerment.

Peace and Blessings,

Coach Lane

References

Brown, B. (2010). *The gifts of imperfection: Let go of who you think you're supposed to be and embrace who you are.* Center City, Minn.: Hazelden.

Jeffers, S. (1987). *Feel the Fear and Do It Anyway.* New York: Random House Publishing Group.

Rohn, J. (1993). *The Art of Exceptional Living.* Simon and Schuster.

Williamson, M. (1992). *A return to love: Reflections on the principles of a Course in miracles.* New York, NY: HarperCollins.

About The Author

Lane Cobb is a Speaker, Transformational Author, and Spiritual Life Coach committed to helping women create more joy, freedom, prosperity, and authenticity in life.

Creator of the "Intuitive Body Coaching Method", Lane helps women connect with their divine essence and make right choices, so they can live their purpose and fulfill their rightful destiny.

With over 25 years of experience, Lane is a sought-after expert in the fields of transformation, motivation, and healing, and is an example to women who seek to ignite their passion, live their purpose and achieve their greatest potential.

In her book, "Heal Your Power, Heal Your Life", Lane provides women with a simple plan for bringing healing and personal power into their lives so they can love and accept themselves unconditionally, express themselves authentically, and live their best life.

Lane shares her expertise in ontological healing technology, body-mind-spirit continuum education and emotional intelligence, to help her clients develop motivational strategies for optimizing personal and professional performance.

To learn more about Lane Cobb's products, programs, and services, visit Lane@LaneCobb.com

Embrace Your Power!
Achieve Your Potential!
Live Your Best Life Now!